TURKISH TAPESTRY

A
Traveller's Portrait
of
Turkey

HOLLY CHASE

BOSPHORUS BOOKS

1993

Library of Congress Cataloging-in-Publication Data

Chase, Holly
Turkish Tapestry / Holly Chase

ISBN 1-882443-00-4 CIP 92 74019

1. Turkey — Travel and social commentary

I. Title.

For permission to reproduce selections of this book or to order any of our publications, please contact:

BOSPHORUS BOOKS
P.O. Box 3452
Groton Long Point
Connecticut 06340
U.S.A.

Printed in the United States of America

Interior book composition by
Pinnacle Publications; Noank, CT 06340

Cover design by Donna M. Cristadore

Table of Contents

Table of Contents

ACKNOWLEDGEMENTS

"He travels fastest who travels alone."

—Rudyard Kipling

"Who travels alone without lover or friend,
But hurries from nothing to nought at the
end."

—Ella Wheeler Wilcox, in reply to Kipling

Writing this book has been an act of love. *Turkish Tapestry* could not have reached the reader's hands without the support and encouragement of many individuals, some of whom helped me long before I'd even thought to write a book of this sort.

To my fellow travellers—scholars, tourists, pilgrims, nomads, unflappable bus and taxi drivers—thanks for your wisdom, cheer, and quick reflexes. Legions of artisans, merchants, cooks, and innkeepers have shared with me trade secrets and the fruits of their labors. In the dark labyrinths of their collections, patient librarians have held candles for me. I am grateful to gatekeepers, night-watchmen, and muezzins—those who, both literally and figuratively, hold keys to Turkey's great monuments. They have helped me pass through many a door.

When I lived in Ankara in the 1970's, many Americans extended hospitality that was truly Turkish in its scope. Elsie and Nessim Shallon invited me for long lunches overlooking the Kavaklıdere vineyard, while the Masts and the late Tilmer and Rae Engebretson trusted me as their house-sitter. Intrepid travellers and cherished companions, Martie and Paul Henze opened their Land-Rover, library, and home to me.

Altan Zeki Ünver, of The Development Foundation of Turkey, accepted me as a volunteer consultant in handicraft marketing. My work for the Foundation led me into the villages of Anatolia, which remain forever fixed in my affection.

Imaginative and dependable, Zeynep Arda Baykal and Tosun Bengisu, attended to all those details that made travel carefree for the tour members we introduced to Turkey.

Acknowledgements

Art historians Walter Denny and Larry Butler (who, dressed as the subject of his thesis, Haghia Sophia, wore a paper dome and minarets to a Halloween party) have enriched my travels, and thus, this book, with their eloquent erudition and camaraderie.

Wayne Myers has given me, a recalcitrant technophobe, countless hours of patient, lucid, and light-hearted instruction in the mysteries of the word processor. And tapping out my thoughts, I've kept in mind my ideal reader, Emily Myers, a companion with whom I've shared so many Oriental, if not yet Turkish, delights.

More than anyone else, Birsen and Sinan Sinangil are responsible for my comprehension of Turkish culture. For an unforgettable and continuing lesson in hospitality, I shall always be in their debt.

Introduction

I feel I have never given a convincing answer to that persistent question: "What first got you interested in Turkey?" I can offer only this list of possible, and seemingly inconsequential, starting points:

1) Music; minor keys—*Scheherezade*, "Anitra's Dance" from *Peer Gynt*. (When I was four, I would perform what I called "my snake dance.")
2) The one-page "Turkey" entry in a child's encyclopaedia: "Turkey produces attar of roses..."
3) The scene in Louisa May Alcott's *Rose in Bloom* when Rose's uncle, back from Constantinople, presents her with a steamer trunk of Turkish costumes and a box of Turkish delight.
4) The peacock-feather fan in Ingres' *La Grande Odalisque*; a reproduction of the painting hung in the living room of one of my aunts.
5) The Camel Cigarette tin in which my mother kept odd buttons.

When I was eleven, I produced a little watercolor depicting domes, a minaret and a flying carpet—no doubt inspired by my *Arabian Nights* readings. (Allowed unrestricted run of the public library, I took on the Burton translations when I was too young to wonder at their salacity.) I cannot offer any more forceful explanations for my leanings East.

"Your parents just let you, when you were only eighteen, go off alone to Turkey?" That's the other question.

In the autumn of 1971, I was one of thousands of young Americans travelling around western Europe and living off earnings from the previous summer's employment. That I'd wanted, for years, to go to Turkey was not reason enough to go. I needed a mission, and I devised one: to observe and write about the festival of Whirling Dervishes, held each December in the central Anatolian city of Konya. I had a student's interest in comparative religion, especially in Islam and Oriental mysticism. Though not intending to make the journey by myself, I was unable to persuade any of my friends to leave their year-abroad programs in Florence, the high

Renaissance, or Vivoli's *gelati* for the uncertainty of whatever lay beyond Byzantium.

It was a time of cheap student airfares... I was already half-way across the Mediterranean... My parents didn't "let" me go off to Turkey. Alone and apprehensive, I simply went.

During my first Turkish sojourn (and in every one since) Turks proved helpful and extraordinarily hospitable. After shocking the Tourist Office in Istanbul with my plans (A) to stay in a Konya hotel (definitely "not done" by single women, young or otherwise, in Konya in 1971) or (B) to pay room and board to a local family ("no decent family would accept money from a guest"), the Office arranged that I would be the guest of a Konya bank manager whose daughters were studying English.

When I arrived in Konya, the banker, who spoke no foreign language, panicked. With me sipping orange juice in his office, he phoned the bank's largest depositor and suggested that this curious girl be his guest. Within ten minutes I had been packed into a Mercedes and driven at life-threatening speed through Konya's winter dust to a small modern apartment building. Inside a marble foyer, I entered an elevator that rose two floors before its doors were opened by an attractive, smiling woman in her late thirties. Behind her I could see a comfortable room furnished with Turkish carpets and French furniture.

"Oh," she said in excellent English, "you must be our guest! And how long will you stay?"

I was stunned.

This is how I came to be part of a Turkish family, that of Turhan and her husband, Kenan, as I call them in the following pages. (Out of respect for their privacy, I have deliberately sketched Turhan and Kenan's portraits in plain graphite while using more color to depict the people around them.)

Friends kind enough to have read and commented upon my manuscript say I ought to include more information about myself. Though flattered by their interest, I have chosen to oblige my readers' curiosity only partially. It is my wish to focus on Turks and Turkey, not on the adventures of a presumptuous, though well-intentioned, foreigner.

In the early years of getting to know the country, Ankara was my base of operations as I supported myself by buying and selling nomadic and village weavings as well as other handicrafts. The pursuit of these items, which I periodically lugged back to sell in the States, led me over dirt roads to remote hamlets and through many a bazaar. Such outings comprised much of my "field work." Though my initial and primary interest had been to spend as much time as possible in Anatolia, both my business and my academic interest in Islamic art grew to the point that the carpets I had hoped would always transport me back to Turkey began to confine me to the U.S.

Though I have not abandoned trade, in recent years I have devoted much more time to planning and running a few small cultural tours to Turkey. Rather than sell a client an object, I would prefer to share Turkey, the part of the world that has given me my most rewarding experiences.

And here I must stress that one of the most enjoyable aspects of Turkish culture is its cuisine. Like the traveller in Turkey, the reader will encounter images of food—gardens, fields, markets, kitchens, and tables replete with the bounty of the land and the skills of its cooks. For me, it has proved impossible to put all the food on a single plate, to serve it up as one unified course—or chapter. There is simply too much of it. If it has become one of the pervasive themes of this book, that is because food is a medium of the Turks' artistic expression and the leitmotif of the hospitality they have so generously extended to me.

I've not written *Turkish Tapestry* in an attempt to demystify an exotic land and its inhabitants. Turkey is characterized by contrast, contradiction, and convolution—the prerequisites for endless fascination. To my mind, these attributes invite questions as satisfying as any answers. I would like this book to do the same.

Holly Chase
August 1992

Notes on Turkish Pronunciation

Modern Turkish is written phonetically. Stress falls equally on most syllables, though a final syllable may receive extra stress. Though Turkish shares many sounds with English, there are a few important differences:

a as in "father"; followed by *y*, it is pronounced like the English "eye."
c like *j* in "jelly"
ç like *ch* in "chance"
e as in "met"; with *y*, as in *bey*, it sounds like the English long *a* in "say."
g always hard, as in "go"
ğ lengthens preceding vowel. Ex: *yoğurt* nearly rhymes with English "court."
h always aspirated
i as in "kit." Ex: İstanbul
ı (undotted) like *u* in "sun"
j like *s* in "pleasure"
o as in "no"; followed by *y*, it is pronounced as in the English "coy."
ö as in German; or like the English *u* in "curl"
ş like *sh* in "shell"
u as in "lure"
ü like *eu* in "entrepreneur"
y as in "yet" or to lengthen preceding vowel

When two consonants occur together, each is pronounced separately: *Meh-met*, *mih-rab*, *muhab-bet*, *tek-ke*

To simplify the few examples of Turkish plurals, I have used an unitalicized English "s," in place of the harmonic Turkish suffixes.

1

The Cutting of Flowers

Kenan shifts the Land-Rover into low gear as we climb the rutted road leading to İsmet's house, a barrack-like cement building with dogs lazing about its foundation. As we arrive, a servant runs out to greet us. Then he stands waiting for someone to tell him what to do, for there are no horses to tie up.

"*Selam aleykum*," he says, "İsmet Ağa is shaving."

"Come," says Kenan to me, "we'll go to cut some gladiola flowers." We walk to the far side of the ugly building and come to a garden, mostly flowers bedded out in the Victorian fashion, borders of Sweet William (which the Turks call "Sweet Hüseyin"), petunias, and roses—all fragrant in the early sun, the dew not yet gone. Stepping over parsley, we reach a sunken bed filled with hundreds of gladiola, green swords rising from the earth.

Perhaps forty or fifty of them show blossoms, or at least buds. It is late June, the season has just begun. "This part İsmet plants for his friends," explains Kenan. The servant jumps down, about three feet, into the bed. "Just a few," we tell him. The man cuts a pale yellow stalk, fully opened, then a short coral spray, then a violet one. He hands them up to me one at a time as he cuts.

İsmet appears, his shirt untucked, feet in sandals, face pink from the razor. He and Kenan are close friends; there is no need for the litany of polite greetings. He smiles at me and asks, "*Ne var, ne yok*? What is, what isn't, what's up?" It is not yet eight o'clock, an unusual time for a visit.

Turhan is Kenan's wife. Yesterday her mother died. The funeral will be today in Istanbul at the Şişli Mosque, and it is Kenan's duty to tell this to anyone who would want to honor the memory of a member of his wife's family. İsmet has no phone, so we have come ourselves. "She died after her noontime prayers," says Kenan, a Muslim, but not a religious man. We all stand, silent for a moment before İsmet notices his man amongst the gladiola. He calls out to him, "*Kes*! *Kes*! *Kes*, *Paşa*! Cut! Cut!" He calls his servant "*Paşa*" in the way of the old families, who bestow grandiose honorifics on their elderly retainers. Again: "*Kes*!" The word has the sound of a knife slicing through a succulent stem. "*Kes*! More, more! Get that white one and the pink beside it. No, that hasn't enough buds. The yellow is a beauty, take it! You've missed the ones along the wall. Gather those, too. They'll open nicely." The servant is cutting as fast as he can. *Kes, kes, kes*, the hiss of the blade.

"Enough, brother, enough!" calls Kenan.

And İsmet replies, "What good are they here? *Kes*! Don't forget the reds in the corner!" The servant gives me an armload of blooms and goes back to work. "*Kes*! For the love of Allah, take them all!" shouts İsmet, not so much to his man as to his fields and horses and forested hills. There is scarcely a bud of color in the plot now.

"*Tamam, Paşa*." The servant's arm falls slack and he gives me his last stems. We all return to the Rover, where I place the bouquet on the back floor. "Shouldn't we have a wet cloth to lay over them? It's a long drive to the city," I say.

"No need, they're suprisingly hardy." İsmet has switched to the aristocratic English he learned as a youth, "I loathe funerals, positively loathe them. What a sad ending for your vacation. Have you ever been to a funeral here?"

"No, but I'll go today."

"So shall I. Perhaps it will be interesting for you," he says flatly, "to learn more about life here."

And death, too? Yesterday, when I'd asked Kenan if I should bring flowers to the mosque, he'd answered, "No, Islam is a simple religion."

Kenan has the motor running. İsmet bows to me from his shoulders, "Until later." I climb into the passenger seat and wonder what we shall do with the gladiola, our bright and robust cargo.

My years in Turkey: thousands of impressions as vivid as the blooms at my feet this morning. The flowers thirst for water, my impressions for ink. Before they fade, the gladiola will brighten the family salons. Hushed by heavy velvet upholstery, those rooms are always dark, even in happy times.

In preserving my bouquets, I am confronted by too many leaves and petals to press in closed diaries and dictionaries. So, I seek the open page. As the Turks say, what you give away you keep.

2

In Essence

But why choose Turkey? In answering, I suffer the frustrations of a lover wishing to be original, or at least clever. What can any lover say of love that has not been said before? What can I write of Turkey that has not yet been written about somewhere else—from Marrakesh to Kashmir, from Cap d'Antibes to Khartoum? Like the other territories between those points, Turkey, too, is tracked with history. It, too, boasts brave races and wondrous landscapes, wild and tame. Are the steppes of Asia Minor less harsh than the Spanish meseta, the Toros ranges more spectacular than the Sierra Nevada or High Atlas, the Euphrates as storied as the Ganges, the white-washed Turkish Aegean villages as charming as the island hamlets whose Greek flags wave in the winds from Anatolia?

What lies at the heart of this country? What, besides language, defines the nation we call Turkey, the core that remained after the Ottoman Empire had been pared away?

Its people.

"Geography and history, the two co-ordinates of the development of any human society, stand out in Turkey, establishing the place and the moment with unique clarity, and the imaginative traveller can see not only a land and a people, part strange, part familiar, but also a living past and thus himself in history."

—*Discovering Turkey* by Andrew Mango, 1971

For over five centuries, Turkey has been a sovreign power, its own boss. Since the end of the fifteenth century, the majority of territory lying within its present-day boundaries has suffered no foreign ruler. And for even longer, Islam, that egalitarian religion whose name means "submission," has dominanted Turkish society. In tandem, these conditions have forged an enduring self-confidence, but a confidence unalloyed with arrogance. If Turks now rarely effect the cultural hauteur and disdain to which other imperial powers subject each other and their former colonies, is it because they have little need for such airs? Few alive can recall the Turks losing face on their own turf. (Their World War I defeats in the distant Arabian sands were less significant than their local victory at Gallipoli, and they remained neutral in World War II.) Turkish soldiers' fearless, unsparing ferocity in battle never shed its renown, and their repeatedly successful repulsion of home-threatening enemies maintained national pride that withstood even the crumbling of their empire. Were wars (at first, for territorial gain and, later, for defense) what allowed the Turks to be such languid, mannered gentlemen at home?

> "...what was truly Turkish about him was the physical repose with which he confronted the world... The Turk has a monolithic poise, an air of reptilian concentration and silence. It is with just such an air that a chameleon can sit, hour after hour, upon a shrub, staring unwinkingly at the world, living apparently in that state of suspended judgement which is summed up by the Arabic word *kayf*."
>
> —*Bitter Lemons* by Lawrence Durrell, 1957

Did those periodic expenditures of male agression, distant campaigns in Hungary or the Crimea, ensure the uninterrupted percolations of *nargile*s in cafés along the Bosphorus? When Turks today eschew cultural bombast, is it because they can afford to? Few modern nations have the luxury of such a collectively uncriticical (and sometimes naive) perception of their own history.

Could the Turks' legendary hospitality have bloomed so lushly in any a climate save one of unviolated security? Or apart from a religion that exhorts its adherents to magnanimity? Despite Turkey's official secularism, the centuries-bred humility of Islam still tempers its self-assurance. *Jeunesse dorée* who have never prayed in a mosque will nonetheless preface casual plans for a disco date with the word "*İnşallah*, God willing." This is not blasphemy, merely custom, subconsciously respectful of continuity.

Without its people? The country could still bewitch with its natural beauty and variety. And while Turkey's archeological treasures, drinkable wine, favorable exchange rates[†] and relative, if recent, political stability[††] make it inviting, it is not

[†]Prices quoted in the inflation-plagued Turkish lira reflect rates in effect at various times during my two decades in Turkey.

[††]The text of this book had been completed before the 1990-91 Gulf War and the collapse of the Soviet Union. Important as these events were, their effect on most of the people and places I describe has been slight. Thus, I've chosen to let my original commentaries stand rather than rewrite certain chapters (on the Kurds, for example) in a futile attempt to keep pace with nightly newscasts.

the only land claiming those attractions. What distinguishes Turkey from other nations is that, as the concentrate of a pluralistic empire, it is a truly mature society in which tradition orders but does not crush or stultify. I love the Turks for their courtesy and deliberate dignity, crystallizations of the tolerance that springs from their own diversity.

The Ottoman Empire absorbed rather than stifled that diversity. In most instances, it made "Turks" out of Albanians, Persians, and Yemenis only after it had drawn them to its heartlands—the Thracian and Anatolian territories that are now the geopolitical reality of modern Turkey. Empires, like most phenomena of history, repeat themselves. A Roman citizen, say, an Alexandrian or Ephesian who had never resided in the capital on the Tiber, would ever remain a provincial. Romanized as the littorals of Africa and Asia Minor certainly were, geography and local populations determined that their settlements would never mirror the Eternal City. Would the saying "When in Rome..." have evolved if life there had been the same as life in Palestine or Iberia?

The transformation of Macedonian or Transylvanian Christians into Muslims could be accomplished in the span of a life, as when young Balkan boys were given, sold, or drafted into the Sultan's Janissary corps. But to be a Turk, one really had to be born into an already Turkified household. Anyone, an Egyptian or even a Russian, might become an Ottoman, acquiring the requisite modes of speech and conduct, for the the Empire was a meritocracy in which Christian-born slaves could rise to the offices of admiral or grand vizier. An ethnic minority in their own empire, the Turks regarded the espousal of foreigners as strengthening, not diluting, their bloodlines. Eventually, Turkishness came to depend less on heredity than on acculturation.

> **"(We take our) color from Allah, and who is better than Allah at coloring."**
>
> **—Surah II:138, *The Koran***

Outside North America, Turkey has the most varied physiognomy of any place I know. Late in the twentieth century, faces of Turkish nationals hint of empires, alliances, invasions, commerce, and convenience. Are the red hair, freckles, and blue eyes of a Malatya shepherdess traces the Norman

Crusaders left among the swarthy Kurds? The pert hotel receptionist says one of her great-great grandmothers was a slave from the Sudan. All those Istanbul blonds! Are they descendants of Serbians culled for the Ottoman army, of Circassian concubines gathered in the Harem, of German girls swept off their feet by contemporary Turkish *gastarbeiter*? The Tatar family sipping tea beside the stream: waxy, translucent complexions, like white jade; auburn or light brown hair; green or hazel eyes enfolded by epicanthic lids; high cheekbones. The boys are named Cengiz and Timur....

Often as these faces appear, they are but candied fruit in the cake. More pervasive are the classic features the West already "knows" from Edwardian illustrations for the *Arabian Nights* and the *Rubaiyat of Omar Khayyam*: pale skin, dark hair, slightly slanted eyes. But today one almost never sees the smooth cheeks and wispy beards of the first Turks and their Mongol cousins. The nation's men owe their luxuriant moustaches and five o'clock shadows to Mediterranean, not Central Asian, bloodlines.

In profile, the flat-backed skull of a newly-shaved Anatolian army recruit is as characteristic as his olive drab uniform in scratchy wool. And I recognize Turkish women by their sensuous feet, by the little pads of flesh at heels bared and pressing against the wedges of house-slippers or the straps of stiletto sandals.

The bodies of a nation develop their own architecture. Atatürk's cantilevered eyebrows, the arch of a dancer's foot—physical extremities reveal ethnicity. Finials of flesh and bone, heads and heels let the traveller know better where he stands.

In my first days in Konya, before I had learned to cover my head like the local women, people stared at my unevenly sunstreaked hair. In central Anatolia, away from the cosmopolitan cauldrons of the coastal cities, natural blonds are less frequent, and, at that time, the blond highlighting techniques of Istanbul hairdressers had yet to penetrate the hinterlands. "I do not understand," said a kindly man with rudimentary English, "is your hair black or yellow?"

3

Istanbul

"What is your work?" the bookseller asked me.
"I'm a professional dilettante."
"Oh, you mean an Orientalist!"

—conversation in the antiquarian book bazaar
Istanbul, 1986

"I am always at a loss to know how much to believe of my own stories."

—Washington Irving

Taken from Greek, its very name means "to the city," and it has always drawn people. Once and forever it pulled me out of the familiar, and became, more than any other place, my town. That I have never resided there for a span any longer than a few weeks is immaterial. Istanbul is a home for my heart.

Like many travellers, I went there first on my way to somewhere else. In my case, that was to

Konya for the Whirling Dervish Festival. Twenty-one years ago, I arrived in Turkey on a one-way ticket. I have never really left.

Istanbul. In those early days I pronounced it Istan-BOOL, the French way, because it sounded more exotic. How little I knew about the place when I landed there without maps, guidebooks, or local currency. (It was Sunday and even the airport bank was shut.) I had one word of Turkish, involuntarily learned from my seatmate on the plane when he decorously handed me his card and informed me that he was a dairy wholesaler from Tehran. Printed in inscrutable Persian and Turkish, but familiar French, were the words for "cheese."

As a child, I had dreamt of an Istanbul redolent of incense and shimmering above the Golden Horn, which I imagined as a sun-drenched inlet shaped like a real cornucopia. Later, Art 1 introduced me to Haghia Sophia ("...the greatest domed space in the world, forty-one feet higher than the Pantheon...."); I heard about the sumptuous wares of the Covered Bazaar and read that Turks sprinkled their desserts with rosewater. In other words, I was ripe for the disillusionment that came as soon as I boarded the bus bound for the Turkish Airlines city terminal. Wailing and static emanated from the dashboard radio; the inside air was blue with acrid cigarette smoke. We drove into town past miles of dilapidated concrete factories and apartment buildings. Simply unfinished or partially destroyed by some calamity (an earthquake? bombs?)—the source of their dereliction was unknown. Having just left Florence, I felt this ugliness most acutely, and seriously considered going straight back to the airport. But that would have been giving in. I was eighteen, undefeated. I forced myself to stay.

During the next twelve hours I was carried through the city in old DeSoto taxis and befriended by Talyan, a middle-aged sports writer on a right-wing newspaper. First, I installed myself in a very basic hotel of his recommendation. Then he took me out to dinner at a fashionable Bosphorus restaurant and asked me to marry him after I had innocently volunteered that I knew how to make stuffed grape leaves. His English, though stilted, was clear, and his message unmistakable. "Please give me your answer tomorrow," he said. "I know you are too far from where you live. You may need some time to think. My mother and father would like to see you. In the evening, you can come for meeting them in our home." He drove me back to my hotel and said good-night with grave formality.

My lodging was a place for businessmen without expense accounts. As far as I could tell, I was the only woman there, perhaps the only one who had ever been there. A bath and shower were down the hall from my room, but I was wary of the dimly-lit corridor that evening. Indeed, sometime past midnight someone tried the handle of my door, which I'd been careful to lock. Though it was probably only someone who had mistaken my room for his own, I remembered the words of my favorite French teacher when I'd told her of my plans to visit Turkey. "*Ah, cherie*," she'd admonished, "*attention à la traite des blanches*!"† This new sensation, of being in a completely foreign environment, was unnerving. Confusing the English words "too" and "very," Talyan had said, I was "too far" from home. And he was right.

The next day I visited Haghia Sophia and felt appropriately reverential standing amidst the shafts

†"Beware the white slave trade!"

of light lancing through its dense space. But the adjacent Blue Mosque was not blue enough and smelled of socks. Simultaneously engrossed and repelled by this quarter of the old city, I spent the entire day roaming its streets. Sheep followed flannel-bloomered peasant women past mutton carcasses hanging in butcher shops, while dwarves hawked lottery tickets beneath posters of lasciviously plump cabaret singers. Diesel fumes mingled with the aroma of roasted sesame. Men stared at me and spat on the pitted sidewalks; I didn't know if the staring and the spitting were connected. No one spoke to me, and I was overcome by the city's cacaphony—klaxons, bells, jangling horsecarts, motorbikes, buses, porters growling under their loads, tea vendors rattling metal saucers. And beneath it all, running like water down a drain, Turkish—soft, guttural, unfathomable.

Skewers of meat and onions, earthen crocks of yogurt, stacks of puffy bread, bouquets of parsley, pyramids of rice *pilav*, plates of fruit, and trays of syrupy sweets were invitingly arrayed in windows of restaurants I was chary of entering. (There was nothing, except "cheese," that I could say to anyone....no women sat in the fluorescent-lighted eateries...was the food safe?) Finally, because I could peel them, strip away whatever contamination they might carry, I bought some tangerines off a pushcart. As I ate them there on the street, the fragrance of their rind floated above the odor of horse manure. Afterwards, I stood in the Hippodrome and contemplated the Egyptian Obelisk by dusk.

When Talyan picked me up at the hotel that evening, he was the only person to whom I'd spoken to all day. Beneath a blazing chandelier, we dined at his home with his parents (corpulent and placid at either end of a lace-covered table) and a bland couple from the British consulate. The Englishman declined the apples and oranges passed at dessert. "Never was one for fruit," he said. "Weakens the insides."

"My parents liked you too much," said Talyan as we drove back to my hotel. "And they are too happy if you will join to the family." I said something to the effect that I could never consider marriage without my parents' consent. "Then you must return to America and be asking their permission. May I kiss you good-night?"

Wondering if I had been trapped in a foreign phrasebook, I answered, "No, but thank you too much for a lovely evening." He sighed, asked me to remember his proposal, and gave me a business card with both his home and office phone numbers. We shook hands, and I let myself out of the car as quickly as I could. Hospitable, naive, and courteous in the face of rcfusal, Talyan left me feeling bewildered and graceless. I never saw him again.

Before leaving Istanbul, I allowed myself to be lured into a small shop whose sidewalk hucksters promised, in half a dozen languages, sheepskin coats at cheap prices. The garment I bought is the only thing I have ever been "sold," but I was a willing victim. I had heard that Konya would be very cold; besides, I'd long wanted a sheepskin coat. It was too tight from the start ("Buy little small, will become stretch," the salesman had said.) and smelled hoofy on damp days. But it was stylishly cut and kept me warm long after that first Turkish winter.

I had spent two days on the European side of Istanbul before departing on a morning bus for Konya and the dervishes. On a ferry-deck packed with cars and goats, the bus crossed the Bosphorus to the Asian shore. I looked back at the edge of Europe, at the receding city whose minarets pierced mists dissolving in the strengthening sun. Somewhere between the banks of two continents lay the point from which there was no return. Instinct told me that failure to pry myself away from the West, then and there, would probably keep me forever from the East. Afraid that I had bitten off more than I could chew, I nonetheless convinced myself to let the journey take me, even if I had misgivings about taking it. Disraeli said, "The East is a career." Although I did not know it then, I had already begun mine.

Over the next few weeks, Turkey was spread out at my feet, like carpets in a shop. My Konya family gave me a heady introduction to their culture, and invited me to return; I promised I would. I kept my word and learned to speak theirs—Turkish, the language of many delights. After a few more visits, I came to live and work in the modern capital city of Ankara. But I avoided Istanbul. The scene of my first culture shock did not beckon, and even though I had returned there a few times, the city and I had not proved compatible.

On one all too memorable occasion, I was the dinner guest of two businessmen hoping to export hand-beaten copper vessels to America. At the restaurant I asked for wine, which never arrived; my hosts and their wives ordered *rakı*, the fiery anise-flavored liquor that clouds when water is added. Loathing the drink, I took a few small sips, to be polite.... I clearly recall the belly-dancer atop our table and then nothing more until late the following morning when I awoke, bruised and very ill, in an unfamiliar apartment in the working-class neighborhood of Fatih. Standing over me was the moon-faced wife of one of my hosts. She put me in a taxi that took me back to my (then) frugal and campy hotel, the Pera Palas. Deciding I would contemplate my disquieting experience in lodgings that had seen better days, I sheepishly moved to the Hilton. I still don't believe I could have drunk enough of that distasteful spirit (which the Turks call "lion's milk") to have erased fourteen hours from my consciousness, but I swore off *rakı* forever.

Associating the city itself with my discomfiture, I contrived to stay out of Istanbul for three or four years, until fog forced the landing of what was to have been my direct flight to Ankara from Europe.

The airline put up the passengers in a hotel much like my very first. Though we checked out early enough, it was only to languish in the smokey domestic terminal (an apt noun for the passenger holding areas of certain Middle Eastern airports). Fog and violent trade union disturbances delayed our take-off from my metropolitan nemesis, but we eventually escaped. Such encounters certainly contributed to my feelings that Istanbul deserved to be treated less as an intimate than as a suspect acquaintance.

My Turkish friends could not comprehend my antipathy for their celestial city. Since the spring day in 1453 when the Byzantines succumbed to the Ottoman forces and Sultan Mehmet, kneeling in Haghia Sophia, consecrated it as a mosque, Turks have been nurtured by the ideal of Istanbul. Nomadic warriors, they captured not only a city but a civilization. The city's praises have long been extolled in popular songs; and throughout Turkey, in places as far-removed from Mediterranean cosmopolitanism as towns along the Iraqi border, one is not surprised to see the signboard of an Istanbul Drycleaners or an Istanbul Kebab Salon. As a name with which to conjure, Istanbul is more puissant than Paris.

Istanbul

To shun Istanbul was to do no less than refuse to drink from one of the well-springs of the Turkish soul. At least that is how my friends saw it. And so one summer, I set aside five days for the sole purpose of coming to terms with Istanbul. This time, on my way to nowhere else, I went to the city accompanied only by books—stories of the city and guides to its mosques, churches, caravanserais, fountains, bazaars, and markets.

I walked miles through the very alleys that had first made me feel foreign and explored neighborhoods whose lanes bore names like Street of the White Moustache. I stayed in a good hotel and indulged myself in the tempting foods sold on the streets and in the countless restaurants. Yes, I had a little more money than previously, but more significantly, I had Turkish. A language acquired by accretion as much as by study, it gave me confidence and the ability to please the most casual Turkish acquaintance. This time, when the city spoke to me, I answered back.

One afternoon as I was walking across the Golden Horn on the Atatürk Bridge, a car slowed along the sidewalk and its driver called to me in accented English. "You know the road to Europe, please?"

Startled, I answered, "This *is* Europe." Where are you going?"

"France." The car, like so many others that summer had Lebanese plates; the battles in Beirut had begun the year before. A Kleenex box labelled "Hospital of the American University of Beirut" sat on the front seat.

I felt a pang for that city and that lovely campus, where I'd once spent a week. "I think you want the E-5 highway, but I don't drive here and can't explain exactly how to find it. I know it's over there, though." I pointed across the Golden Horn.

"Where are you going? To that part?" he asked. I nodded. "Come, I drive you." Remembering my own first time in Istanbul, I felt an obligation to help. I got into the car...because of the Kleenex box, I think. The driver was an Armenian electrician on vacation, and he wasn't fleeing Lebanon, not yet anyway. He drove me to the mosque I'd intended to visit. "Would you mind if I came in to see it with you?"

We entered the mosque of Rüstem Paşa. The August afternoon was prematurely grey, dark as

November, so I asked the attendant to switch on the lights. The illumination bounced from the glassy wall tiles with their brilliant reds, blues, and greens. The only visitors, we walked about together admiring the decoration of tulips, meanders, *çintamani* spots and stripes. I picked up a strand of chartreuse plastic prayer beads from a windowsill and fingered them idly as we strolled.

When the Armenian said he had to be going, he asked if he could drop me anywhere. I told him I planned to continue my explorations on foot. He thanked me for showing him the mosque, and we went outside to put on our shoes, which we'd left at the door. Before we parted, I wished him—as well as his city—all the best.

It was not until months later that I found the prayer beads at the bottom of my camera bag. At one point during the visit to the mosque, perhaps while adjusting a lens, I must have set them down atop the unzipped bag. Over the years I've had numerous opportunities to return them to Rüstem Paşa; and yet I've kept them, treasuring them in the spirit in which they were given. While another Levantine city was at war, Istanbul and I made our enduring peace.

Eventually it dawned on me that I had, after all, accepted that first proposal of marriage. My union was not with a forlorn sportswriter following right-wing soccer teams, but with his country, especially with his city.

THE ASIAN SIDE

"I am listening to Istanbul, intent, my eyes closed;
Still giddy since bygone bacchanals,
A seaside mansion with dingy boathouses is fast asleep,
Amid the din and drone of southern winds, reposed,
I am listening to Istanbul, intent, my eyes closed."

—*I Am Listening to Istanbul* by Orhan Veli Kanık (1914-1950) trans. by Talat Sait Halman in *Contemporary Turkish Literature*

Villages strung along the Asian shore, I tell their names like beads: Beykoz... Küçüksu... Kandilli... Çengelköy... Beylerbeyi. More than the physical reality of water, it is reflection, both littoral and spiritual, that separates these settlements from the frenzied commerce and intrigues of The Other Side. Slumbering beneath the plane trees that shade the coast road, the towns are slow to awaken, especially in summer. Cafés deserted until mid-morning await the clatter of backgammon pieces. A white-scarved woman sprinkles water to cool her sidewalk, and the rising vapor has the unmistakable pavement smell of diesel and dust. From a side street comes the resonant cry of a vendor balancing a tray of fresh sesame bread-rings on his head: "*Simit*!"

Farther down lies ancient Chrysopolis, old Scutari, contemporary Üsküdar with its sad hospital haunted by ghosts of the Crimean War—cholera and gangrene victims even Florence Nightingale couldn't save. But as if in consolation, every sunset gilds the eastern shore of the Bosphorus. Remember that Chrysopolis means "city of gold;" and silk-napped Scutari velvets once rivalled those of Venice. Fair competition for the painted sky behind the silhouetted domes and minarets of old Stamboul across the water. Besides, one of Üsküdar's royal mosques has this: an inscrutable placard admonishing that "It is forbidden to throw cats from the windows."

In the district called Harem, the wizard-hatted towers of the Selimiye barracks loom above the bus station. From here one leaves for Istanbul's unchic, inland Anatolian suburbs. And for Ankara, Aleppo,

Baghdad, Mecca—a different rosary. The independent bus companies have their offices in a row of little glass store fronts, and each window is graphically lettered to suggest speed. The forward-slanting script makes good use of arrows, flames, and serifs fluttering like pennants. The carriers' names are *Tanrı Verdi* (God-given), *Yıldırım* (Lightning), and *Güven* (Reliance). Some simply use surnames; the star among those bound for Konya is *Özkaymak* (Real Cream).

Just below the confluence of the Bosphorus and the Sea of Marmara lies the Haydarpaşa train station. At first, the building appears to have as little depth as stage scenery. Open to the elements, it serves to separate the train platforms from the ferry dock, where travellers drawn (or pushed?) farther east are finally culled from the masses anchored to their city.

With its pointed arches and turquoise tile mosaics, the ferryboat reception kiosk on the Haydarpaşa quai seems displaced in this maritime setting. But then this is perhaps less the water's edge than it is a continent's, a point of departure for the Asian expanse whose vastness mocks Europe and the comprehensible Marmara. So, is it not fitting that Haydarpaşa should hint of Tabriz and Samarkand and caravanserais far from every sea while the vaults of its ticket hall echo with the flapping of confused pigeons?

4

Anatolia

OF SOULS AND STOMACHS

"Geography, according to the new view, tells us not only what forms of plants and animals live together in mutual dependence, but also why the human inhabitants of a given region possess certain habits, occupations, and mental and moral characteristics, and why they have adopted a certain form of social organization."

—Introduction to *The Pulse of Asia*
Ellsworth Huntington (1907)

The perfect cone of Hasan Dağ rises against a few puffs of cumulus and a sky almost as blue as the mountain itself. Below lie the only amber waves of grain I know. I've never seen America's great grasslands, but I recognize this extension of the steppes of Central Asia as the heartland of the country my heart has chosen.

Anatolia

It takes a wide-angle lens to encompass the Anatolian Plateau. Here, photographs taken with a normal lens are diminished in majesty; only optical distortion makes the landscape look right, the way I see it, even without a camera. The little red poppies and full-headed grain at my feet and the stones in the sheepfold half-way up the distant slope seem in equally sharp focus, a neat trick. Mystics, monks, and dervishes have dwelt here for centuries. Surely, they have been bred by this plateau, where one need only raise a hand to touch the sky?

During my first visit to Turkey, precipitated by the annual festival of the Whirling Dervishes in Konya, I wrote little. At that time my energies and attention were completely consumed by the unfamiliar; each night I fell into the heavy sleep of a traveller enriched and fatigued to the point of dreamlessness. Only after I'd ended that intense, inital sojourn and made several others was I able to consider Turkey in the ways I now write about it.

"The food is cooked; the spoon is planted on top."
—Turkish saying to signify that "all is ready."

As the capital of the Selcuk Turks, Konya drew the traffic of caravans, which gave the city not only material wealth but also a leavening of cosmopolitanism.

When Marco Polo passed through Konya, he wrote of its fine carpets, though not of its food. Hailing from the silk-weaving and trading entrepôt of Venice, which had mastered the culinary use of Eastern spices early on, he might himself have noted, in Konya, the felicitous coexistence of the skills of the shuttle and the spoon. It has long been my experience that cultures displaying accomplishment at the loom excel, too, at the hearth.

Contemporary Konya's Museum Street was once an arm extending from the cruciform intersection at the center of Roman Iconium. Now it leads to the green-tiled mausoleum of Celâlettin Rumi, thirteenth-century founder of the Mevlevi sect, popularly known as the Whirling Dervishes. This main thoroughfare is lined with kebab eateries, carpet sellers, and other shops replete with the books, costumes, and tacky souvenirs of the dervishes. Gold-lettered Korans and volumes of mystical poetry, posters of Arabic calligraphy, reed flutes, and locally made brown felt fezzes stacked like flowerpots are jumbled with figurines, postcards, and lurid headscarves printed with images of Rumi's tomb. These shops also sell a variety of pointed wooden spoons.

Most of the spoons are larger than what Westerners would consider appropriate for the table, and with their capacious bowls, they seem more suited to stirring soup than eating it. The spoons are hand-carved, graceful with their tapered handles and pointed bowls like cupped leaves. The foreigners prefer the plain ones, the Turks those with Arabic script, tiny red flowers, or other motifs. Nearly all the spoons are heavily shellacked so that their decoration can withstand use. But no one would think of sullying those painted with pictures of the mausoleum or turbanned Rumi himself. Like most saints, Rumi would probably rend his shroud over the veneration and commercialism surrounding his final resting place. But he might, perhaps, take a gentler view of the Turkish spoon cult, especially apparent in Konya, where the tomb of his own chief cook, Ateşbaz-i Veli has just been restored.

The landscape around Konya has long fed more than souls. The central Anatolian pastures, wheat-fields, and orchards have provided the basis for much of Turkey's superior cuisine. If the Turkish attention to gastronomy ever needed moral justification, one could always turn to examples set by the dervishes; their charitable institutions included hospitals, where doctors prescribed curative diets of special foods, and kitchens, where hospitality was extended to wayfarers and paupers. As implements of benevolence, spoons themselves have acquired a sort of sanctity.

The Mevlevi, famous for their consciousness-altering dance, came largely from well-educated, aristocratic levels of society; they developed a sophisticated body of devotional music and poetry that strongly influenced other dervish orders and Turkish literature. Although they sometimes practiced asceticism, the Mevlevi were sensualists whose embrace of this world was but a metaphorical expression of the bliss they sought for their souls. In their intellectual and emotional striving for union with God, the ecstasy induced by music and other earthly delights was both a path to God and a foretaste of God's love itself.

In literature as well as practice, Muslims, like Christians, have frequently utilized food and drink as symbols of spiritual nourishment. Coffee or alcoholic beverages were sometimes used in dervish ceremonies. In addition to stimulating or relaxing the body, these liquids played a more powerful role in representing the waters of Paradise, which would quench Man's thirst for knowledge of God. Rumi, the mystic, bids us remember that:

> "The Man of God is drunken without wine,
> The Man of God is full without meat."
>
> —*Divani Shamsi Tabriz*, trans. R.A. Nicholson, 1898

Cooking, not only to sustain, but also to please, became an act of devotion, as the flavorful kebabs, *pide*, and butter-based dishes of Konya admirably attest. Dining with friends, eating from a common dish with one's own spoon, is analogous to the quest for enlightenment. Though he joins in the rituals of the dervish *tekke*, or convent, the individual alone is responsible for feeding his body as well as his soul. Though a member of the community, he must find his own way to God.

> "If you plan to eat *aşure*, carry your own spoon."
>
> "What you slice into the pot comes out in your spoon."
> —Turkish proverbs

When, to commemorate the martyrdom of the Prophet Muhammad's grandson, Hüseyin, the dervishes would prepare *aşure* (a delicious pudding of wheat, beans, nuts, and raisins), members of a *tekke* would take turns stirring the mixture with a great spoon. Turkish pudding shops now sell *aşure* year 'round, but when housewives make it in remembrance of Hüseyin, they, like the dervishes, prepare it in huge batches so as to be sure of having enough to share with their neighbors. Meanwhile in Konya, where the modern Whirling Dervishes are "officially" mere players in an historical reenactment of traditional dance ceremonies, yard-long spoons hang in the souvenir shops. And the tourists are told they are giant salad servers.

Then there are the Konya spoon dancers. Troupes of them travel the country and perform at festivals, Istanbul nightclubs, and in tourist hotels. Young men and women, moving in a line parallel to onlookers, step back and then forward and occasionaly form circles. One wonders if the dance is in any way derived from the lines of dervishes who chant and sway shoulder to shoulder. But as Anatolian dances go, this is a little dull—except for the spoons. In each hand raised to shoulder-height, the dancers wield pairs of spoons placed back to back: Turkish castanets, more tricky to manipulate than their Spanish counterparts. Spoons carved from hard, fine-grained Turkish boxwood (what Dürer preferred for his engravings) produce the clearest sound.

> **"When the food has boiled over, the ladle is worthless."**
> **—Proverb**

If only for its name, one must mention the Spoonmaker's Diamond, the great jewel of the Topkapı Palace treasury, which legend says an old woman bartered for a dozen wooden spoons.

> **"Whoever turns away from the *pilav*, may his spoon be broken."**
> **—Proverb**

Surprisingly, this is not an admonishment to those who refuse second helpings, though (in Konya, at any rate) there must be a saying that chides the guest who fails to do justice to his host's table. Rather, this proverb carries the sense that one should not spurn the opportunities that come his way. Luckily, the inexperience and uneasiness of youth could not dull my appetite for what Turkey set before me on my first visit. I shall always be glad that even though the *pilav* has often been overwhelmingly rich, I have kept a place at the table. My spoon remains whole.

THE KONYA FARM

"Rain for the farmer, drought for the traveller;
God will grant everyone his wish."

—Turkish proverb

Privilege. July at the farm outside Konya. Bees hum among the yellow plums and apricots fallen in the orchard. Their aroma mingles with the grass Lütfi scythes in the yard; the slice of his blade is just audible. There is no lawn-mower, and this green plot is not a deliberate lawn, only grass that has been allowed to grow in the shade of a locust. I float in an icy irrigation tank—or swimming pool, depending on one's point of view. Of grey cement, it holds water pumped from the farm well. It takes nearly two days to fill, and even in midsummer the water stays cold for a week. We use it to chill melons. There is no filtration system, so every seven days, before it breeds algae, the unchlorinated water is drained into the irrigation ditches of the orchard.

In this conservative agrarian province, where few know how to swim and hardly a woman would be caught dead in a bathing suit, I float, half-naked, enjoying the water before it is returned to the dry earth. Practical privilege. What an easy indulgence for a guest: understanding without accountability, the luxury of detachment. Though I don't know it yet, today my dozing has left me lying too long in the sun. Tonight I shall sleep with the pleasant heat of a sunburn, yet to peel or freckle my chest for life. From a minaret in the town, a breeze bears a muezzin's mid-day call, sacred above reddened flesh.

After lunch I read coffee cups for anyone who's here, but never more than three cups in all. (I lose my touch, I say.) But I'm a bit chagrinned when the maids take it so seriously; I should have known better. Now they eagerly await my daily prognostications, which I reveal in French, far better than my Turkish during this particular sojourn. The children attempt to translate for me. The servants listen gravely, especially Fatma Hanım, who helps in the house despite her bad knees. She has asked us to save apricot pits so that she can plant trees for her daughter's dowry.

The Turkish poet Nizam Hikmet writes that

"You must take living so seriously
That even at seventy
You will go out and plant trees—
And not so they'll be left for your children either,
But because even though you fear death,
You don't believe it,
Because living weighs heavier."

—from *On Living*, trans. by J. Michael Lowry

Because I am stronger than she is, Turhan asks me to carry the heavy pails of her apricot and cherry preserves upstairs to the sleeping porch. Each pail weighs about twenty pounds and must be carried by its wire handle, which I wrap with a cloth so it won't cut my palm. The stoned fruits have been boiled briefly with nothing more than sugar and a little water, and now they are suspended in a heavy syrup that will be further reduced by evaporation. I lug the pails up the narrow pine staircase and set them down on the floor of the balcony with its carpet cushions. At night when the beds under the eaves are too warm, this is a cooler place to dream. But for several hours each day the sun owns the spot. To keep out wasps, we cover the open pails with cheese cloth. Over the next few weeks, the sun will concentrate the flavor of the jewel-like preserves. I am glad to assist in this distillation of summer.

> "The only athletic sport I have ever mastered was backgammon."
>
> Douglas Jerrold (1803 1857)

They have taught me to play backgammon in their languages—Turkish and French. Ever after I shall call out the dice in Turkish *(altı, bir; üç, dört)* and speak of ill-fated pieces as *cassé*. Turhan, who breathes upon her dice before she rolls, seems unbeatable. Her rings sparkle as she flicks her wrist with each deft throw. I ask her if winning is a question of cleverness or luck. Luck, she says. Kenan, kibbitzing from the side, says it's cleverness, adding that one must watch out for Turhan. "*Elle triche*," he states flatly.

The Turkish name for the game is *tavla*, and there is a verb, *tavlamak*, which means "to trick." Loaded dice are said to be "pregnant."

After dark we suspend our play, cease slamming the pieces on the wooden board. There are few mosquitos as we sit outdoors around the short-wave radio that picks up the BBC from its nearest broadcasting point, Nicosia, or Lefköşe, as the Turks call it. Television has not yet come to Konya. I tickle Turhan's daughter, Esma, as she squirms in my lap. Kenan's cigarette glows as we wait for the little air announcing the World Service Broadcast. No matter where I hear that melody, it unfailingly evokes all the nights at the farm, and one night in 1974, when we are straining to hear Nicosia's static-riddled report of Turkish military maneuvers on Cyprus. As I write these words, eighteen years later, there is still no solution to the tensions in the waters washing Cypriot, Greek, and Turkish shores. The eastern Mediterranean continues to bear the burdens of its turbulent history.

Detachment has its darker side: the outsider must sit on the sidelines of contests fought with rancor more deeply rooted than the gnarled olive trees clinging to the rocky coasts.

GREEN HARVEST

"A fig tree is best inherited from one's father, but an olive tree best inherited from one's grandfather."

"If you have honey in the pot, bees will come from Baghdad."

"Grass is soft, but Allah is greater."†

—Turkish proverbs

When streams rush with melting snow, shepherds begin to move their flocks to upland pastures, and migratory beekeepers follow with their swarms in blue wooden boxes. What the palm-fringed oases of the desert are to the Bedouin, the *yayla*, the high verdant fields of Anatolia, are to the Turks. Abloom with clover, alyssum, mint, anemone, and scores of unnamed flowers, the *yayla* is the Turks' paradise on earth, a real land of milk and honey—and cheese and butter. Extolled in song and verse, the *yayla* is where the fresh winds of spring blow away the stress of long winters in confining towns and villages. Settled peasants in solid houses, schoolchildren in

†I haven't the faintest idea what this one is supposed to mean.

black and white smocks, skinny sheep in mud-caked fleeces—they all long to return to green grass.

No people rejoices more at the coming of spring than the Turks. And I think they celebrate not only the spring of a given year, but also the spring of their history. Is it because they began as nomadic herders and warriors untethered to the soil, that they seem never to have exhausted what must have been their first delight in greenery sprouted from seeds they had sown themselves?

In the towns, spring arrives with the pushcarts of *can eriği*, "soul plums." Small, round, hard, and bright green—they have a crunchy, tart flesh said to be the passion of Turkish ladies. Many people would judge them unripe, as indeed they are. The few that are not devoured in spring stay on the trees to turn into yellow fruit. But later, when the plums are ripe, so are dozens of other fruits and vegetables. It is when there is little else to challenge them that they offer their choicest, most craved flavor.

Because of its feathery foliage, asparagus is called *kuşkonmaz*, "birds won't light upon it." Istanbul restaurants celebrate the asparagus season with numerous dishes that make the most of the short-lived crop, though no one disputes that the green spears are best simply drenched with browned butter....

In the eastern province of Van, far from the effete hollandaise sauces of Istanbul, people eat raw, wild rhubarb shoots, which look like asparagus that has begun to bolt. Even with an ecumenical interest in gastronomy, I find *ışkın* weedy, at best. Van also has *otlu peynir*, white sheep's milk cheese made with wild herbs and spring onions. In the dairy bazaar rise yard-high mounds of this local specialty, the original "green cheese."

For at least two-thirds of the Turkish year, all delight in sweet hearts of romaine lettuce. In a wineglass of lemon juice, the tender chartreuse leaves are the perfect centerpiece on any table, be it napped with oilcloth or lace.

On early summer nights along the Bosphorus, sisters of the gypsy rose-sellers peddle green almonds on trays of crushed ice. Calling "*Taze badem*, fresh almonds," they saunter along the corniche, pausing sullenly before our outdoor table until one of us purchases a scoopful of almonds. No matter what the stage of our repast, we turn our attention to their unhardened, velvety shells the color of jade. Splitting them open to extract the immature nuts and slip off the wrinkled husks into which they've not yet grown, we savor the milky white flesh and kernels of clear jelly. Their taste, of almost spiritual purity, is young and, well, green.

Filiz, borrowed from the Greek, is a popular modern name for a girl. Meaning "bud, sprout, shoot, tendril," it is a delicate, green name. A feminine variant of "chip off the old block"?

Rug dealers often say that green is rare in Oriental carpets because of its sanctity as the color of the Prophet's banner. But might not the color be rare because it was once difficult to dye, and could that in turn have made it sacred? No single plant or mineral available to the wool-dyers of old would yield a permanent green. Before the middle of the nineteenth century, when synthetic dyes were first introduced to the Middle East, a green textile dye always required at least two dyeing procedures—one for blue and one for yellow. And as the fabric aged, the top-dyed yellow often proved to be fugitive, with the result that only a greenish blue was left where once had been a true green.

What of the souls of the sultans and dervishes who lie in elegant green-roofed tombs? And the back-street saints whose gravestones and shrines have been daubed the greens of crayons and municipal swimming pools?

Praise be to Allah for the other greens: pines scenting the shores, pollarded willows drinking from streams, silvery olives, flooded rice, seas of new wheat, rows of sugar beets, truck-loads of parsley and watermelons. In the Konya province, a rank of poplars—planted when a girl is born—mark the boundary of her parents' field, shade their seedlings, and grow strong withstanding years of wind. When the girl marries, they become the roof beams of her new home. A true proletarian, genus *Populus*, the most ubiquitous of Anatolian trees, provides wood for spoons as well as cooking fires. In contrast, the huge old *çınar*s of Istanbul, cherished for their cool shade and beauty, are indolent aristocrats. Outside the Booksellers' Bazaar near Istanbul University, grows one surrounded by rickety tables of gossiping tea drinkers. It's a *Platanus orientalis*, but they call it the Tree of Idleness because its shade is so conducive to repose.

> **"A tree's at its best when it has leaves. A person thrives with friends around him."**
>
> **—Turkish proverb**

> **"A goat that climbs a tree has a kid that eyes the branches." (Children learn from their parents.)**
>
> **—another proverb**

Whether from mercenary legions' undoused campfires or fractious gods' lightning bolts, some of Anatolia's ancient forests undoubtedly died by fire; but most fell for the navies of great powers: Phoenicians, Romans, Ottomans. Along the Mediterranean coast, drought-tolerant pines and holm oak now struggle against the predations of Mephistophelian goats. Remember that these scrub-covered spines of hot white limestone once gave Süleyman the Magnificent masts for the Battle of Lepanto and Cervantes his oar in a Turkish galley.

In summer, clay pots of tiny-leaved basil sit on windowsills. Surprisingly, the herb's culinary use is almost unknown here. It is popularly supposed to repel ghosts and insects, and ladies ruffling its foliage with their palms enjoy the scent as they would a splash of cologne. A sprig may be given to a departing guest, for remembrance.

5

The Language and the Looking Glass

"...a traveller who knows something of the world, and of God, and desires to travel quietly, must have a sufficient idea of...language to understand whether good or evil is intended to him, whether they are going to offer him bread or a box on the ear."

—*Seyahatname* of Evliya Çelebi, 17th century†

The desire to extend my friendship to Turks made me consider learning German, since so many I'd met on my initial visit to Turkey had that as a second language. Fortunately, the ridiculousness of that idea soon hit me—why not learn Turkish?! As it turned out, I could not resist the invitation on the

†Evliya Çelebi's *Seyahatname* (Book of Travels) is a colorful record of his journeys throughout the Ottoman Empire. In particular, his descriptions of 17th century Constantinople provide historians with tantalizing details of urban Turkish life.

first page in my first of many copies of one redoubtable little book—

> "Turkish is a member of the Turkic branch of the Altaic family of languages, spoken ... from the south-east of Europe to the borders of China. Its structure is simple and logical, and it has now discarded the Arabic script in favor of the Roman alphabet. This book presents the Turkish language as it is generally spoken in present-day Istanbul... As the languages of the Turkic branch do not differ much among themselves, anyone who masters the contents of this book should find little difficulty in making himself understood in Adrianople, in the Turkish-speaking parts of Cyprus, in Chinese Turkestan or Samarkand."
>
> —*Teach Yourself Turkish* by G.L. Lewis, 1953

Arriving in Turkey from the neighboring lands of Greek, Cyrillic, and Arabic script, the innocent, Western eye rejoices in the shock of the familiar. Written in the Roman alphabet since 1928, Turkish, with its phonetic orthography, seems disarmingly accessible. What could be simpler than "*foto*" or "*taksi*"? But the rules of word sequence introduce the would-be conversationalist to the sortilege of this language. It is not only the verbs lurking at the end of sentences (the way they do in the "less alien" disciplines of Latin and German), rather, it is the whole bag of tricks, with its changeling gerunds and possessive suffixes, that will madden or bewitch the student.

The most pleasurable intellectual endeavor of my life, learning this language has proved to be a vaccination eradicating the lingering malaise of recurrent tourism. It grants resistance to dishonest taxi drivers and pestering postcard peddlers. Once inoculated, one can roam freely, almost invisibly, to watch and listen. Turkish has given me what I most value—my lofty status as a fly on the wall.

> "Some hold translations not unlike to be
> The wrong side of a Turkey tapestry."
>
> —*Familiar Letters* by James Howell (1594?-1666)

It is a law of nature here: no matter how long he dwells in Turkey or how sympathetic he is to its society, the Westerner retains his foreignness. In time, of course, he is less frequently overcome by the sensation of having tumbled down the rabbit hole. Yet he will never cease to notice the small, ordinary things that seem askew or reversed.

To indicate "no," Turks do not shake their heads from side to side; they jerk them back. The unaccustomed often infer arrogance or indifference from the gesture, which may be accompanied by raised eyebrows and tongue-clicking. In fact, all this body language is a simple "no." (Even Turkish two year-olds refusing to eat their vegetables toss back their heads and utter little "tsks.") However, most of the confusion results from the muscular relaxation that follows the action—a nod that does not mean "yes." While the physical language has no particular head motion for the affirmative, in written and spoken Turkish, the negative is emphatic, doubled to leave no doubts. When "no one is not home" or "nothing is not left," it is advisable to come back later.

A Turkish friend notorious for the gloom of his prognostications defends them by pointing out how happy people are when things turn out better than they'd dared hope. Which of his kindred spirits wrote Turkish Airlines' emergency safety instructions, which advise passengers to use their seat cushions—not "for flotation" but so as "not to sink"?

✷

TURKISH TAPESTRY

"...they filtered you through the mirror of the city"

—from *First* by Sezai Karakoç (b. 1933)
translated by Murat Nemet-Nejat
in *Contemporary Turkish Literature*

In a typical antique shop—among the Damascus backgammon boards, rosewater sprinklers of milky Beykoz glass, and dubious icons—will be at least one old mirror. There should be just enough tarnish to enhance the beautiful chasing of its elaborate silver back. Round or oval, ten to fifteen inches across, it will hang from a chain and lie flat, its glass turned to the wall...

A fine silk prayer carpet made in Hereke is adorned with borders of Arabic script. What do these magnificent letters exhort or invoke? Nothing divine, they are but the opening lines of Turkey's (completely secular) national anthem. But even if one reads Ottoman Turkish (which the vast majority of today's Turks cannot do), the script is legible on only half the rug. In line with the Islamic love of symmetry, half is executed in mirror-writing.

In mosques whose congregations lean towards Sufi mysticism, austere wall decorations of Arabic calligraphy are painted in mirror image to form designs for contemplation. An ornament may consist of a single letter like the hissing "s" or hollow "u," whose repeated vocalizations are used in the hyper-ventilation that can lead to altered consciousness.

By eliminating many of the Arabic and Persian letters that figured in the Ottomon language, modern Turkish has radically simplified its orthography. But as a consequence, homonyms abound. Even though I'm fully aware that there is no etymological connection, I like the coincidence which allows the contemporary word *sır* to mean "the silvering of a mirror" as well as "secret; mystery."

6

Accommodations

LUNCH

The *Guide Bleu* mentions Eğridir only in passing, because that's what most tourists do: pass it on the way to somewhere else, someplace with fallen columns or rock-cut cuneiform or luxury hotels. The lack of such attractions notwithstanding, the town is definitely "*vaut le voyage*." Though the crammed iconography of stars, crossed cutlery and bathtubs has yet to be applied here, it is only a matter of time.

West of Konya lie the lakes where the Selcuks retreated from the summer heat of the plain. Like dissolving sandcastles, the sultans' pleasure pavilions rim waters as limpid as the Caribbean. The treeless, unpopulated landscape is gaspingly beautiful: aquamarine lakes set amidst jagged mountains, snow-crested even in June. The splendor is other-worldly, as preposterous as color slides from two different holidays (to the Bahamas and Switzerland?) serendipitously stuck together to form a montage in one slot of the projector tray.

From wherever one has stayed the previous night, it will take at least a morning to drive to Eğridir, an unremarkable cluster of concrete buildings, cafés and pensions on the shore of one of the lakes. If arriving as I first did, with a small band of fellow travellers, one is wise to telephone or write ahead so that the management of the best restaurant has time to prepare its full array of hors d'oeuvres, its myriad *meze*.

Out of the mid-day glare, in the deep shade beneath the broad awning, one focusses on a long buffet table set with twenty or so cold dishes. But first, to wash. One must enter the restaurant, built around an enormous *çınar* tree growing straight through a hole in the roof. But the Eğridir Restaurant has other wonders. This is still a part of the world where one does not take plumbing for granted (even in excellent restaurants), so the attractive, immaculate, and perfectly functioning facilities come as a much-appreciated surprise.

Refreshed, one proceeds down the cold buffet table spread with black and green olives; pickles; sweet cucumbers, green chili peppers, and plumes of romaine lettuce; cracked wheat salad; cheeses; anchovies; lake-caught crayfish; grape leaves, peppers, and tomatoes stuffed with cinnamon-tinted rice and currants; buttery yogurt with garlic and spinach or beets; separate dishes of baby eggplants, zucchini, broad beans, white beans, and artichoke bottoms bathed in olive oil and lemon juice. The regional specialties are supplemented by a few gustatory classics from the old empire: Albanian-style liver—sautéed, sprinkled with paprika and chopped purple onions; pastrami cured with fenugreek; Circassian chicken in walnut sauce; and my disarming favorite: pale, silky lamb brains with lemon and parsley. The all-essential bread waits at one's place. Besides frosty beer, a waiter offers the local wine in an unlabelled, corkless bottle that reveals only its color, golden like the beer. Fruity but dry, the cold wine is delicious and more than a little alcoholic.

Catching welcome breezes off the lake, the dining tables are practically on the sidewalk, where boys sell bottled rose water and rose skin-cream in pink plastic jars. Eğridir is not far from Isparta, famous for its heavy-scented roses grown between orchard rows of apples and pears. The boys are soft-spoken and polite, proffering their inexpensive wares with restraint. To recapture the sweetness of Turkey, I can think of no better souvenir than their rose water, which is pure enough to splash on one's face or sprinkle over compotes of summer fruit.

A return to the buffet seems over-indulgence even after a fragrant intermezzo of gentle bargaining. Yet it is hard to resist one more spoonful of Circassian chicken or a floweret of pickled cauliflower... Well, maybe just one more small stuffed pepper... Sighing, one settles back in the chair. Smug because one's party are the only foreigners in the place, sated by the impeccably prepared food, and soothed by the wine, one is disbelieving (aghast might be a better word) when the waiter appears shouldering a platter of perch. "*Doydum*, *doydum*! I'm full!" one protests. And protests in vain, for the honor of one's country depends on measuring up as a diner.

"But it is our specialty," says the waiter as he presents the hot fish on a fresh plate. "You must take some." One is helpless. "*Afiyet olsun*, *bon appetit*." He watches as one takes the first taste. The fried filet's delicate shell shatters at the touch of a fork. Steam swirls around a morsel en route to one's mouth. Let it cool for a few seconds, ask the waiter about the perch itself. Native? From this lake? "Yes, some Swedes stocked the lake a decade ago. A development project. Now eat."

One obeys. Turkish tempura? Devastatingly good, it tastes like nothing else prepared by this country's skillful fish chefs. Of course, the waiter knows this and beams. "A little more wine?" With the third bite, one makes a silent promise: next time, only ten *meze* but *two* perch filets...

REPOSE

If, after such a meal, little nap seems in order, Turkish has *the* word: *şekerleme*. Perfect for the post-prandial forty winks, it also means a small candy or bonbon. The quintessential after-dinner mint.

But how strange that the siesta is not an official institution in Turkey! And so the unfortunate tourist, like that hyperactive Hellene, Alexander, feels compelled to press on across Anatolia.

Aegean İzmir, remembering the more languid Greek population that, until the 1920's, enriched its society, is the only Turkish metropolis to shut its shops mid-day. In cities that endure hotter summers, merchants pretend to stay open all day. Yet despite the ministrations of the coffee and tea boys, on summer afternoons every bazaar dozes. The din of the tinsmiths subsides and the cloth-merchants, assuming the disposition of their stocks, drape themselves amongst the flannels and ginghams that cushion their slumber.

But if one really wanted to sleep softly, he would seek out the quilt-makers' bazaar, where men stitch seed-flecked cotton filling between layers of heavy muslin. At this stage, a quilt looks like dimpled *pide* bread, risen and ready for the oven. Next, the quilts, many of which are made to order for brides' trousseaux, are covered in bright, glossy satin chosen by the buyers. Favorite hues—maroon, chewing-gum pink, and aqua—enliven the open stalls, where, even on winter evenings and under naked bulbs, the workers sit sewing with great needles. Their threads follow decorative patterns, compass-drawn, like giant snowflakes.

TURKISH TAPESTRY

"Peace shall go sleep with Turks and infidels."

—William Shakespeare; *Richard II*,
The Bishop of Carlisle in Act IV, Scene I

With an arm drawn across his face against the summer sun, he has fallen beside a country road, or, if he is lucky, in the shade of a solitary tree in a field of wheat stubble. A corpse, I once supposed. But no, he is a farmer or a hired hand deep in the unabashed slumber of physical exhaustion. At work since before dawn, he breaks in late morning for bread, cheese, and cucumbers. He swigs water from an unglazed clay jug and sleeps off his repast as if he had drunk a liter of the very wine forbidden by the Koran. Trucks rumbling along the asphalt are as much a lullaby as the day-long drone of cicadas. No one sleeps more profoundly than a Turk.

"She brought forth her firstborn son, and wrapped him in swaddling clothes..."

—The *Bible*, Luke 2:7

Enveloped in shawls and made fast to their mothers' backs or rocked in cradles and hammocks hung with amulets, the infants of Anatolia are tradition-bound in yards of cotton swaddling. In the old days, the ultimate pacifer, a knob of opium-laced candy might be tied in cloth and given to soothe teething or colicky babies. Bobbing above tiny cocooncd bodies, the babies' drowsing heads, often in blue-beaded and embroidered caps, hint of the children who, like butterflies, will one day emerge, if Allah is merciful.

When the hot weather comes to the steamy plains of Cilicia, gauze sleeping tents appear on the flat roof-tops. They are white, semi-opaque fabric, fine enough to foil mosquitos, stretched around and across the tops of squares created by quartets of upright poles. At bedtime some glow softly, like Japanese lanterns, for candles are often lit within. Children succumb to story-telling, husbands and wives to each other. One by one, as evening yields to night, the cubes of light are extinguished.

Tunics of puckered, hand-loomed cotton are cut low at the neck, revealing the pale cleavages of nursing mothers or the comforting, curly mats on the chests of their menfolk. Depending on heat, shyness, and simple preference, either sex may also wear loose calico or striped drawers to bed. With the pre-dawn call to prayer, these garments and the half-conscious bodies in them stir from the roof tents, an encampment of semi-somnambulists. Before the sun hits the television antennae, before the motorbikes assault the senses, the mauve, mute beauty of this auroral society belies our century.

HOTELS

Because there are no friends with whom to lodge or simply because one craves freedom from guesthood, there are times when beds must be bought.

Travel is a succession of small triumphs. Catching a train and settling into one's seat or securing a hotel room in a strange city, taking possession of space, even for a night, is a kind of conquest. Closing the door, extracting a toothbrush, hanging up a jacket, opening a book—these are the small privileges of a victor, whether he arrives at dawn after a flight scheduled to disrupt his circadian rhythms or at night after the stimulation, and perhaps frustration, of being anywhere but home.

It was in Turkey, where I could actually afford hotels, that I became a connoisseur of their luxuries, discomforts, and idiosyncracies.

In the provincial hotels (the sort where heat is an itemized charge on the bill) one awakes to the tinkle of spoons stirred in tea glasses and the morning throat-clearings of smokers, businessmen on the road. Room decor usually consists of a uniquely ugly fixture for shedding inadequate light, plastic laminate furniture, droopy curtains, vinyl tile flooring, and concrete walls that should have been painted *any* other color.

Praise be for the hard foam mattresses—cheap, practical, and a godsend to the traveller with a trick back. The bed is made up with clean white cotton sheets—and blankets that should shame this nation of textile artisans. At their best they are merely leaden in both weight and hue. More often, they feature the head of a roaring feline or an unsuccessful (pink and ochre) geometric tribute to the Wiener Werkstatte.

Plumbing works with varying degrees of success. Every toilet sports a wiggly plastic seat embossed with the Turkified French: **LÜKS KALİTE**. Wishful thinking.... In the more basic shelters there is no tub or shower stall, just a showerhead that sprays the entire bathroom; but there's a drain in the floor and a pair of plastic bath sandals beside the bed, useful if the drain is slow and one finishes a shower to discover that the water which ran under the bathroom door is now two inches deep in the bedroom.

Places like this are frequently named for the owner or some unassailable symbol of prestige or luxury. Certain words serve as unintentional tip-offs of grungy decrepitude. Although there are not always alternatives, one is wise to avoid establishments whose names include the words *Belediye* (municipal), *Saray*(palace), *Köşk*(pavilion), and, of course, *Lüks*. I once volunteered to pass the night in my friends' Land-Rover and watch over their gear when the only beds in town were in the *İpek Palas*, The Silk Palace. But a prize for truth-in-labelling must be awarded to one unblushingly awful east Anatolian hotel named *Uyanık*, "The Wide-Awake"!

Nonetheless, rusticity is not always to be eschewed. At a friendly, family-run inn amidst the opium poppy fields near Denizli, one dines beneath spreading branches of a plane tree beside the brook that has just yielded the trout on one's plate. In the two guestrooms of the well-swept farmhouse, the only light is from kerosene lanterns. There is no plumbing to worry about: one simply washes upstream from the outhouses, beneath which a branch of the brook has been channelled.

Certain Turkish hotel experiences resist classification. I've slept in a hemisperical, lavender echo chamber, one of the "moon rooms" at a little motel whose architect must have been a Buck Rogers fan. At another inn I watched staff lug Victorian armchairs and fainting couches down a spiral staircase, lather the velveteen upholstery in a sunny courtyard, and return the furniture, slightly damp, to the guest rooms that evening. A sybaritic swim amidst Corinthian columns sunk in the effervescent waters of a Roman spa is like a bath in warm Perrier. Another spa hotel's bathrooms are supplied only with skimpy handtowels—and enormous hooded, cotton terry robes as heavy as winter coats. Then there are weighty, unforgettable room keys with bronze tags guaranteed to wear through one's pocket before one has left town. One Ankara hotel has appended real goat hooves to its keys.

The variety of sounds to lull one to sleep (or keep one awake) range from frogs celebrating an unexpected rainfall to ferryboat fog horns to a muezzin's final call to prayer. Surely the sweetest good-night I ever received was from the reception clerk who wished me "colored dreams."

Much as I enjoy the Pera Palas and the ghosts of spies who ride in its gilt elevator cage, when in Istanbul, my unabashed choice is the Hilton. Not for its American tourists and eagerness to accept credit cards do I ensconce myself here, but rather for its self-confidant Turkishness coupled with cosmopolitanism. Surrounded by fragrant gardens and sited above the Bosphorus, it is a refuge in a city, however beautiful, that has grown too large, too fast. For an *İstanbullu*, there is no more desirable place for a meeting, chance or prearranged, than the vast Hilton lobby. Merely to be seen there makes one a member of an exalted body, a club whose members include local Society and Money, true, but also archeologists in their only clean khakis, missionaries, and smartly uniformed airline crews. In fine weather the lobby expands as its services for tea and cocktails are extended to the veranda. Savor the privet-scented breeze; sit with a friend and face the Bosphorus full of ships in the late copper light. Order a glass of 505 (the Turkish Campari), and it will arrive accompanied by a dish of toasted chickpeas, nuts, and raisins. If it is June, a bowl of cherries—the dark, sweet Napoleons—will be offered as well. Listen to the languages—percolating Turkish, languid Levantine French, hydroelectric German, Australian English, Saudi Arabic, Japanese... An old Kuwaiti sheik, resplendent in his gold *eygal*, red-checked *kefiye*, and black wool robe, shuffles back and forth the length of the veranda—his evening constitutional.

I love: the smoked sturgeon and melon on the breakfast buffet; the triangular turquoise and cobalt tiles in the shopping arcade; the Hachette bookstore; the beautiful Japanese receptionist who speaks perfect Turkish; the marble bathrooms with instant ice water; the view—tiny furrowed fields and the Dolmabahçe Mosque (looking like a mechanical bank) in the foreground of the Bosphorus and Asia; the soignée chambermaids who each day depart by the front door.

What makes me cringe are the rates, paradise at a price.

7

Bazaars

" ...Allah I stretch my hand to you
Seven Hells, eight Heavens, each has its own way
On each way are a hundred thousand bazaars..."

—Yunus Emre
13th century Turkish mystic and poet

SAMANPAZARI

Haphazard planes of red, the terra cotta tile roofs of Ankara's oldest neighborhoods, pattern this city's northern hills. Atop one slope lies the Horse Market, the At Pazarı, and below it the Straw Market, Samanpazarı. In the open square of the At Pazarı, I have bought a crate of dried İzmir figs layered with bay leaves and have seen a vendor bent beneath a score of chartreuse plastic jugs bunched like balloons. But the horse market died out long before I ever came here. Its hay-scented memory survives in the lively shops of Samanpazarı that sell saddles, harnesses, bridles, bits, brasses, blue beads, bells, and hand-plied ropes.

With its hardware, dry goods, basketry, spice, copper, antique, and junk shops, Samanpazarı is the part of thc city I know most intimately. When I lived in Ankara, it was my place of work. Here I would come, four of five times each week, and buy things to be resold in the States.

People often ask me whether I, as a single female, find it difficult to trade with the men who control the bazaar. I can truthfully say that the greatest difficulty I have ever had is one unrelated to gender: refusing (or accepting!) the sixth or seventh glass of tea offered within an hour. Invariably, I am treated with the diffident cordiality extended to any potential customer, male or female, local or foreign. (I do admit that in a market almost untouched by tourism, where the majority of merchants speak only their mother language, my Turkish does give me the disarming advantage of surprise.) Although capable of ruthless bargaining, I rarely need to resort to it. My relationships with the denizens of Samanpazarı are based on our mutual respect, trust, and understanding of the word "wholesale."

Samanpazarı merchants are eager to ensure repeat trade. Rather than overcharge a one-time customer, a seller is more likely to offer an especially attractive first-time price. They say, "*Siftah senden, bereket Allah'tan*", which can be loosely translated as "a sale to you brings blessings from God." And the goodwill continues should a customer return, or recommend the shop to a friend. Just as the seller tempts the buyer back, the buyer piques the interest of the seller by asking for a "better price" if he buys two or more of something. A discount must benefit both parties, or it will never be given. An astute shopper quickly learns that even in a relaxed environment, where merchants seem to have endless hours to spend bargaining, time is valued. In this bazaar, any browser who offers an insulting quarter of the asking price is immediately recognized as an idle time-waster scarcely worth a good-by. I have come to feel that, as a way to while away an afternoon, haggling is over-rated.

I have long favored certain merchants for commodities ranging from sheep bells to socks—

The tack shops sell an odd assortment of things a farmer's or shepherd's family might require: metal collars whose two-inch spikes guard the necks of sheepdogs from wolf bites; striped grain sacks handwoven from black and grey goathair; and *ellik*, wooden finger-protectors for peasants who still cut their grain with sickles. Sharing shelf space are cheesemaker's rennet and bottles of an obscure tonic. Respectively, their garish labels feature a cow against the Alps and a baby sticking out his tongue.

American friends, importers of handicrafts from developing nations, have placed me on the alert for utilitarian items of good design and quirky appeal. I know they'll go for Turkish mousetraps, wooden paddles topped with delicate hexagonal wire cages. I really don't understand how they work (they lack any lethal mechanism), but they are as charming as mousetraps can be. I see a pair of them hanging outside one stall and ask the shopkeeper how many he has in stock. "How many do you need?" he asks.

"Say, a hundred, maybe more."

He looks at me in disbelief. "Where are you from?"

"Çankaya." I give the name of my Ankara neighborhood, generally considered rather posh.

"You should get a cat."

"I have one."

"Well, what's wrong with him?"

"Nothing. You see, the traps aren't for here. I'm going to send them to some friends in America."

Pause. "And you have so many mice there?"

Clearly, I am not corroborating the stories he's heard of luxurious life across the Atlantic. Nonetheless, after a few teas, I walk down the hill followed by all eyes and a hundred pristine mousetraps—lashed in bunches carried by two boys. Enough to fill two taxis and worth the trouble. Months later they land in the States, to the profound bewilderment of U.S. Customs agents who have already cast a dubious eye on a shipment of dog collars.

"Superstition is the poetry of life."
—*Spruche in Prosa* by J.W. von Goethe, 1819

Among the hardware shops is a tiny place selling nothing but beads. Available in sizes from pigeon's egg to pinhead are handmade blue, white, and yellow glass amulets like those worn against the Evil Eye since Phoenician times. The beads are sold singly or roped in hanks, to be fashioned into protective ornaments for infants, animals, cars, and houses. No charm is ready-made; this shop sells only the raw materials. Strings of plain glass seed beads in many colors are bought by village women who crochet them into the fancy edgings of their headscarves. I draw the stares of a fellow shopper as I buy several strings of olive-sized Evil Eyes, perhaps a thousand blue beads. She is counting out coins for a scarf's-worth of seed beads and asks the proprietor what I plan to do with my quantity. The man shrugs and turns to me. "They're pretty," I say, "and we don't have them in my country."

Her eyes widen and she asks, "But then, *what do you use*?"

Reluctant to reveal our barbarism, I say nothing of wishbones and rabbit's feet, or of fuzzy dice and auto insurance.

Peasants would sell their grandmothers' silver belt buckles, bracelets, and chains to Celal so they could purchase the more prized 22-karat red gold bangles for their women. Sitting before his scales, Celal charged me by weight, instead of by the piece, for the kilos of silver jewelry I bought. The shop, which smelled of tarnish, was low-ceilinged and very dark. But as Samanpazarı shops go, it was spacious; it had at least three chairs. Here I bought

Longines pocketwatches made for the Ottoman market. With their elaborately engraved double silver cases, faces decorated with floral garlands, and Arabic numerals, who minded if they didn't run? In any event, neither time nor Celal stood still. After a long absence from Samanpazarı, I found a large glass-fronted emporium selling aluminum kitchenware where I used to paw through trays of Persian and Cyrillic-scripted coins, carnelian beads, and watchsprings. Neighbors said Celal had sold out.

Most taxi drivers have never heard of the Fuar Pasajı, but one can easily find it by asking for the Opera or the flea market (aptly named the *Bit Pazarı*). In terms of geography as well as social acceptability, the Fuar Pasajı tenants rest between these points, on the edge of Samanpazarı.

Although Rahmi Leblebicioğlu's surname means "son of the chickpea toaster," like everyone else in the Fuar Pasajı, he is a rug dealer. To Ankara's Americans, he is simply "Cheap Charlie." Slyly proud of his sobriquet, he refuses to be undersold, rarely failing to turn over most of his stock before the evening prayer. "When things lie here for longer than an afternoon, I become bored with them," he says. Few of the carpets, saddle bags, cushion covers, and *kilim* fragments that pass through his door are remarkable for any reason, save their prices. "Twenty thousand lira, only twenty thousand lira!" Rahmi exclaims as much to himself as to any customer. "How can anything be so cheap?"

Or so dusty, so stained with lamb fat, or so encrusted with bread dough? Still, his prices are unbeatable. Crew-cut, white-haired Rahmi presides over his kaleidoscopic inventory with equanimity. Anatolian grime, wheat chaff, and lint hang in the air as he and his bespectacled brother unroll the rugs from morning until dusk. (There's a Turkish proverb that says the rising of dust from rugs and the snoring of old men will never cease.) Porters come and go, throwing off their loads, bales bulging with scraps of old clothing and unwashed rugs, something to beef up the dwindling stacks. With every year the odds rise against finding that sleeper, a little dowry kilim with cochineal silk and silver threads or a meaty Konya bed rug with no aniline orange. But like a player lingering late at roulette, one waits for the next bale to be slit open.

In a bazaar like this, one is still magnetized by what has drawn Westerners since the Crusades: spices and cloth. Jerusalem may have fallen to the Crescent, but, for Christian adventurers, cinnamon and silk proved substantial consolation prizes.

The *baharatçıs*, spice sellers, sit behind cerulean canisters of paprika—sweet or hot; ground fine or in chewy flakes. They sell dried beans, marigold petals and true saffron, herbs for infusions, laundry bluing, glittery naphthalene moth-flakes—and henna. Used to color and fortify hair, henna has long been valued as a pigment for hands and feet, particularly for wedding celebrations. One could hardly guess that the shrivelled green henna leaves yield a brilliant orange. It is sold in leaf or powdered form; and every *baharatçı* displays open sacks of at least two grades, one usually touted as "luxe," or *lüks* to the Turks.

A friend of a friend—a foreigner—is famous for his delicious lentil soup. From his spice man, he purchases tiny coral-colored lentils, cumin, and a secret powder. A Turkish lady covetous of the recipe finally persuades him to reveal the mystery ingredient. He confesses that he himself doesn't know the name of it, but that it is the green powder sold by all the *baharatçıs*. Somewhat unnerved, the lady says, "But my dear, that's henna!"

Is it merely coincidence when Evliya Çelebi notes that, in the procession of the Constantinople guilds, the lentil-sellers parade immediately before the henna merchants?

Here is a more orthodox version of *mercimek çorbası* (lentil soup)—

2 cups dry red lentils, picked over for stones and well-rinsed
4 tablespoons oil or butter
1 medium onion, finely chopped
6-8 cups broth or water, depending on
how thick a soup is desired
a bay leaf
3 cloves of garlic, finely chopped
1 lemon
1 egg
Chopped flat-leaf parsley, salt, black pepper,
hot or sweet paprika to taste

In a heavy pot, fry the onion until it is golden in 1 tbsp. of the butter or oil. Add the lentils, bay leaf, and liquid. Bring to a quick boil and then simmer, covered, about 30 minutes or until the lentils are very tender and have begun to disintegrate. Stir occasionally and check to see if more liquid is needed. With cooking, the lentils will turn pale yellow.

Grate the lemon rind and juice the lemon. Beat both juice and rind together with the egg until frothy. Set aside.

Just before serving the soup, fry the garlic, freshly ground black pepper, and paprika until fragrant in the remaining butter or oil.

Whisk the egg/lemon mixture into the lentils and stir for one minute. Do not let it boil. Salt to taste. Ladle soup into warm bowls.

Drizzle a little of the garlic mixture atop each bowl and garnish with lots of parsley. *Afiyet olsun*!

Now that it is legal, one spice wholesaler changes money for the occasional foreigner or the many guestworkers home for summer holidays. Amidst the tea tins and fragrant burlap bags bulging with coriander seed and dried jujubes, he tallies marks, francs, and pounds against the laughable Turkish lira. Bring him hard currency, and working furiously with his pocket calculator, he'll pay a better rate than any bank.

Black Sea aprons smelling of indigo; maroon hip-wrappers for the *hamam*; tablecloths block-printed with Bronze Age motifs; Kurdish head-scarves shimmering purple and emerald; striped wool cummerbunds and shawls; crocheted coin purses for feast day largesse; a bride's ransom of embroidered napkins, towels, handkerchiefs, and cradle covers; crimson velvet wedding dresses heavy with gold and silver—the Kulsoy brothers sell all this to peasants and sophisticates alike. Here is one shop where I am never offered tea—because it might damage the merchandise? Hard to tell with the unsmiling Kulsoys whose greatest magnanimity (a token concession to wholesale) is ten percent off. In the middle of a delicate negotiation, with the goods piled high on the counter, their favorite ploy is to leave for the mosque. Though I begrudge these sanctimonious grumps their take, I love what they sell. The shop is packed to the rafters with enough bolts of handloomed cloth and one-of-a-kind costumes to outfit the cast of a Cecil B. deMille film.

Many items—of museum quality—are not exactly priced to walk out the door. Kept wrong side out, their splendors are hidden until Kulsoy the Elder deigns, with admittedly effective showmanship, to do some unfolding. Haphazard browsing is impossible here. The pity is that the brothers evince no genuine, aesthetic appreciation for what they sell, seeming to care only for what they earn. We habitués wonder if they sit on their stock because they expect prices to rise. Someone says that if the Kulsoys wait too long, their tinderbox of a half-timbered building, filled with all those fabrics, is likely to go up in smoke.

Beneath the sagging awnings sheltering the store-fronts from the bleaching sun, there is, of late, an unfamiliar break in the row of Cloth Street shops. The gap is blackened, like the space from which a bad tooth has been pulled.

From his drafty lean-to stand, Fahri the sock-seller continues to purvey the artistry of hundreds of Anatolian knitting needles. (Every Turkish female over five seems genetically programmed to knit and crochet.) Along with long woolen underwear and elastic corsets, Fahri has an especially good selection of naturally white *tiftik* , or mohair, socks. He hangs a few from the awning of his stall, but most are inside, stuffed into large plastic bags. Turkish socks are always stored one inside the other, flat in pairs. Foreigners are skeptical of assurances that these socks, with pointed toes and sharply angled heels, actually conform to human feet; they could easily be taken for ladies' reticules. (In this part of the world—from the Balkans to Kashmir—knitters do not "turn a heel.") But fit they do, and no hose is warmer. The women who execute the intricate cable, shell, and lattice patterns themselves wear the socks with plastic shoes the colors and consistency of gumdrops. They make brightly figured gloves, too. Conforming to either left or right hands, the gloves' contrasting tips recall ancient manicures, a legacy of houris' hennaed fingers in fluorescent orlon.

Checking the mohair for moth holes (synthetics have their advantages), I make my selections. Like the other shopkeepers, Fahri is loathe to give a receipt, which involves carbon papers and official stamps whilst also leaving a record for the taxman.

But the sock-seller is reluctant for an additional reason: he cannot write. On a pad of paper I carry for just this purpose, I make out my own bill of sale, which I need for my records. At the bottom of the receipt, Fahri makes a graceful mark no less legible than the signature of any bureaucrat. At the end of one visit he proudly tells me that his daughter Hatice has just entered a prestigous university in the States as a premedical student.

"*Maşallah*! May God protect her!" I say in admiration and copy her address from the crumpled paper he pulls from his pocket. Samanpazarı yields endless surprises.

"A stone is heaviest where you find it."

—Turkish proverb

Recep sells wooden spoons, wicker furniture, rush mats, and baskets in one of Samanpazarı's larger shops. One day on his upper level, as I am pulling a basket from a shelf, the old floorboards give way beneath me. I crash through the floor until my arms, bent at the elbow because I am clutching the basket, stop my fall. Seeing my legs flailing from the ceiling, Recep races up the stairs. By the time he arrives, I've been rescued by one of my companions, a strong, quick-thinking American serviceman, who has grasped me under my arms and pulled me up. We all praise God for my deliverance and have a good laugh. Recep sends out for tea. (There are still parts of the planet where the aftermath of an accident does not commence with a call to one's lawyer.) It is not until the following day that I become aware of a few bruises. Having sought my dictionary, I learn that in Turkish one is not "black and blue," but "purple."

The item for which I have nearly expired is one of the beautiful, sturdy market baskets made from chestnut and poplar. Thoroughly taken with their pleasing lines and bark-covered handles, I think of my importer friends. The problem is that Recep rarely has more than three or four of them in stock. As baskets go, they are not cheap, far more expensive than the equally useful (but less handsome) cane baskets made by gypsies. I ask Recep what he would charge per basket if I were to order several dozen of the wooden ones. He says he'll have to talk to the middlemen who bring the baskets from the provinces where they are made. A week later he quotes me a price. "But that's more than what you're charging now," I say.

"Yes, but the basketmakers say that to make as many baskets as you want is a lot more work."

"That's crazy. Don't you think they should give you a better price for such a large order?" I ask.

Recep shrugs helplessly. Like many Turkish shopkeepers, he has never struck me as a particularly savvy businessman, just a cheerful, grizzled tea drinker. "What can I do?" he asks.

"Tell them they'll lose me as a customer with those prices. But if they'll price them so you can sell them to me at—[and I name a figure that today would not even purchase an egg, so much has the lira been inflated], I'll put in an order."

Bargaining through Recep with the distant basketmakers or the middlemen (I am never sure), I eventually agree to order the baskets at a price somewhat below the original quote, but scarcely cheaper than the baskets I've been buying all along, two and three at a time.

When they arrive in Recep's warehouse, he is anxious that I pick them up as soon as possible, since they take up so much space. Taxis, fine for the mousetraps, will not suffice for stiff, quarter-bushel baskets with arching handles. A minibus is still too small, so I reserve a small truck with the transport company I use to ship my goods. Squeezed together in the cab of the full-sized moving van the company actually sends, the driver, his assistant, and I ride to the bottom of the snowy slope that leads to the market. Our vehicle, the largest the bazaar has ever seen, turns out to be too big for any street in Samanpazarı, to say nothing of the twisted lane where the warehouse lies. We park, taking up most of the little trapezoidal space where sheep are sold. My henchmen and I, Recep, his teenaged son, a cousin, and some helpful neighbors form a human chain that hands baskets from the cave-like warehouse, down the slippery street, around a corner, and into the van.

It is seven years since I last shopped in Samanpazarı, so when I return to Recep's, I wonder if he will remember me. In this stronghold of men, I am surprised to find a young, yellow-scarfed woman arranging the merchandise in the shop. She calls to someone in the back, and it is Recep's son. Smiling, he recognizes me at once, introduces me to his shy wife, and runs to get his father from the warehouse. I wander around while I wait. The shop is filled with a wide variety of attractive baskets, some decidely chic, not merely unconsciously beautiful because of their utility. As I admire some graced with grapevine handles and wish they'd been around when I'd had the moving van, Recep appears.

"*Hoş geldiniz! Maşallah*! Welcome! How wonderful!" he exclaims. And then, to my delight and astonishment, he stands on his toes to kiss me on both cheeks.

I praise his industrious daughter-in-law and compliment him on the grapevine baskets. He tells me he now deals directly with the craftsmen, no more middlemen. He says business is good and proudly shows me a cozy seating area, floored with linoleum, that he's set up for his clients.

Wickedly, I inquire, "What about the floor upstairs?"

"Oh, that—, "Recep looks simultaneously pleased and sheepish. "That's still the same."

In my days of merchant scholarship, Samanpazarı was the sedate campus of my undergraduate years. Post-graduate field work took me to the teeming labyrinths of Istanbul, where my studies continue....

THE COVERED BAZAAR

"Grace is given of God, but knowledge is bought in the market."

—Arthur Hugh Clough (1819-1861)
The Bothie of Tober-na-Vuolich

Mustafa was born to the bazaar, if not to his particular trade. After school and before he entered military service, he worked in his father's shop selling furniture. Along with beds, armoires, and standing mirrors were substantial chairs and sofas, arms and bodies upholstered in tufted maroon velveteen, feet concealed by deep fringe. Wags know the style by varying names: King Farouk, Louis the Twenty-Ninth, Muslim Morgue....

Originally, Mustafa's father's family were Arabs, but the lines drawn after World War I left them on the Turkish side of the Syrian border. They continued to speak Arabic at home. Indeed, the clan produced many Koranic scholars...and one paratrooper, which is what Mustafa became in the air force. ("It was my greatest dream," he says.) He had hoped to remain in the service beyond the compulsory two years. But although he was unexcited by commerce, Mustafa was his father's only son, the brother of five sisters who must one day be married and installed in homes of their own. He had responsibilities and ought to be settling down himself. He had to stop jumping out of planes. (There's the Turkish saying that "one's good fortune does not come down from heaven in a basket.") So Mustafa came home to Istanbul, applied himself to the furnishings trade, and got himself engaged. Gradually, Mustafa's father turned more and more of the shop's daily operations over to his son. Mustafa, in the long idle periods known to every shopkeeper, watched the changing aspects of the bazaar the way a sailor does the sea.

What he saw was that a lot of young men like himself were making amazing amounts of money selling old rugs, kilims, and saddlebags, the sorts of things that nomads use because they have no furniture in which to sit, sleep, or store their belongings. Really, it was unbelievable what people would pay for patched things when they could have had brand-new, wall-to-wall carpeting at half the price! He knew his mother would have had to inspect those rags for bugs before she'd ever let such things into *her* house. But Mustafa was also aware that there were fewer newlyweds making down payments on heavily carved, cherry-stained armoires. He told his father he'd like to try selling some old rugs. They wouldn't have to put up any cash; he'd get them on consignment....

It was eight years ago that Mustafa's father agreed to the experiment. Now the only vestiges of their former inventory are a few pieces of dark furniture in the apartment Mustafa bought when he still had a fiancée. If the alliance was a failure (she told him she didn't want to have children), the old rugs were a success from the start. It was not long before Mustafa himself was consigning articles to other dealers. He picked up English and made friends with Americans who wanted to sell his weavings in Indianapolis and Denver. They reordered, paid in dollars, and sent their tourist friends to him. Starting as he had, Mustafa was the first to admit he was no rug expert. But he eventually developed a knowledge of which items came from which tribes and villages.

These days his father, slipping into placid retirement as his daughters marry, rarely comes in. When he does, he usually ends up as a mere shop-sitter, telling clients to come back when Mustafa is there.

I drop by unexpectedly, and Mustafa is embarrassed for not having shaved today; he had not expected many visitors. Like most of the other merchants, he is fasting, and this afternoon the lethargy of Ramazan has settled upon the bazaar. Awake since their pre-dawn meal, men have fallen asleep among the stacks of rugs in their shops. Quickly hailing a hovering tea boy, Mustafa asks me, "What will you have to drink?"

"Oh, nothing, thank you. You're fasting. I wouldn't drink in front of you." He insists, I refuse. He tells the boy, who's been scanning the arcades all day for infidel customers, to bring me a lemonade.

Sitting inside the shop, we visit. Mustafa is teasing and a bit sad. No new sweethearts have materialised. "Don't you have an sister for me? Unmarried? Blond like you?" I wish I did, for he's gentle and very handsome. The boy brings lemonade and I drink it, gratefully in this heat.

A simply dressed foreign woman with a small kilim rolled under her arm, enters the shop. She spreads the rug on the floor, holds up five fingers and says "*Aleman Marka.*" Approximately the size of a large bathmat, the kilim looks new and unused. Its colors are garish, its design is primitive, and its weaving undistinguished. But anything, anything handwoven, is worth at least five German marks—or two dollars, fifteen francs, all legal tender in this territory.

Mustafa grins at me and says in Turkish, "A Serbian tourist. We see a lot of them and they're always trying to sell the stuff from their mothers' dowry chests. They don't have any idea about prices." He rummages in his desk drawer, pulls out a five-mark coin, and hands it to the woman. She eyes it suspiciously; I half-expect her to bite it. She gives it back and repeats her price. Mustafa calls across the passage to a friend, and within seconds another young dealer is talking to the woman in her own language. There is much head-shaking and shrugging. Finally the woman picks up the rug and wanders back into the arcade.

"Well? How much does she really want for it?" I ask.

"Who knows? But she'll come back, they usually do. She's just getting offers now," says Mustafa's friend as he leaves.

"How much would you pay for the kilim, Mustafa?"

"How much would *you*?"

"You mean if I actually wanted it—which I certainly do not." He nods. "I suppose it could be sold here for fifty marks, tops, so I might pay her twenty."

"When she returns, she'll let me have it for ten, maybe less."

"It's a wonder she'd even bother to bring something she's willing to sell for so little. What, besides lunch, can she get with ten marks?" I ask.

"Gold."

"You're joking. For ten marks?"

"You'd be surprised," says Mustafa. "There are some very small, very light pieces—little charms and things, eight and ten carat."

"Made exclusively for the Balkan trade?" But then I've just seen a sign stuck in a neighboring window that says "We speak Catalan." I laugh, for this market will accommodate anyone. And is it not written in the sayings of the Prophet that "he who gains is God's favorite"?

"No, even fourteen carat. And the Hungarians buy them, too," says Mustafa, the seasoned trader, lonely bachelor, and former paratrooper whose grandfathers knew the Koran by heart.

GOLD

"I can stand a great deal of gold." —Henry James

Decades ago when Freya Stark was taking the rough roads through Anatolia, some Turkish ladies told her their name for the new moon, "the brow of thc Prophet." On the shores of the Sea of Marmara, the Sephardic wife of an Istanbul metallurgist taught me that one must always wish upon the first sighting of the slender crescent; and to make a wish come true, one should touch gold whilst wishing.... Perhaps someday one of my friends will defer to my suggestion of a Turkish name for a daughter: *Altınay*, "golden moon."

Consider my grandfather's ring: my mother gave it to me when I was eleven or twelve, and I have worn it on various fattening fingers ever since. Like a cigar band worked in gold, it centers on an oval of twining initals. The back of the shank is bent and cut through, clipped open more than eighty years ago, after a childhood mishap—a boy closing his finger in a drawer. No one has ever gotten around to having the ring repaired. It catches on towels, upholstery, sweaters, and in my hair.

But today, on impulse, I have decided to have the ring fixed. I am in the midst of leading one of my small tour groups on a walk through the old markets near Istanbul University. Leaving them to browse briefly in the Booksellers' Bazaar with its courtyard shaded by *çınar* trees, I dash off to the Covered Bazaar.

Even after all my years here, I am intimidated by the gold-sellers. I have always frequented the antique and bric-a-brac shops rather than the jewelers. To be sure, I have bought huge quantities of jewelry, but always silver—hefty collars, chains, and clanking cuffs that appealed to my taste for ornament in the Prince Valiant vein. No doubt, too, that the costliness of gold helped foster my initial preference for silver. But in contemporary Middle Eastern society, jewelry that is not gold is not really jewelry. Perhaps I am slowly succumbing to that opinion, for lately, I've been lingering in the radiant heat of the gold-sellers' windows. Previously, it has seemed too common (married peasant women with wristfuls of mass-produced red gold bangles) or too touristy (day trippers from the cruise ships comparing Istanbul prices to those in Florence and Cairo). In fact, the cost-per-gram of 22-carat bangles is listed each day in the newspaper, along with prices for other staples—white cheese, oil, sugar, mutton...

How does one choose a gold-seller? Unfortunately, I mistrust my Turkish friends' judgement in both style and price. (It seems they pay more for most things than I ever do.) So I am on my own, and the ring repair is a small experiment. With no time to be selective, I go into the first shop on the right as I enter the gold street. Low-key, without an elaborate façade, it is distinctly unglamorous among the scores of shops that adorn their windows with flocked velvets and mirrors—miniature bordellos. Though its jewelry is not particularly tempting, I like this shop's lack of pretension.

"Good morning. Peace be upon you!" I begin.

"And upon you!" answer the proprietor and his two assistants.

"Do you do repairs?" I twist the ring from my finger and place it on the top of a glass case warmed by the lights within.

The proprietor picks it up to examine the cut. "You'll have some tea?" he asks. A tea boy with his swinging tray pauses at the doorway.

"Actually, I'm in quite a rush and have to meet some people in ten minutes. I'd thought to just leave the ring and return later."

"You have time," he says, gesturing that the boy should serve tea all around. I take a glass, but return the accompanying pair of sugar cubes to the tray. This raises eyebrows in a country where virtually everyone takes at least one cube. "If you're rushing," says my host, "you need sugar for strength."

I smile and explain that I never take sugar, "even in coffee." This remark brings a chorus of "ahhh's". There's a Turkish saying to the effect that only old women and businessmen drink their coffee straight.

"Would you prefer coffee then?"

"Another time. The tea is just right for now."

Our attention turns to the ring. "You want it smaller? Bigger?"

"No, only soldered and straightened out, please."

The gold-seller goes to the door and calls out to a small boy across the street. The boy scurries over and is given my ring with instructions to hurry to Aziz the Repairman and to be back as fast as possible. The child disappears into the throng of shoppers. "It should be ready in ten minutes," says the jeweler, noticing that I have finished my tea.

"Another glass?" I decline, explaining that I have an additional errand but that I shall be back in ten minutes. "No problem. The ring will be waiting for you."

I plunge into the bazaar in search of some cheap gold sandals to wear that evening. (Around every corner in Istanbul, it seems someone is always selling shoes.) I quickly find some that are available only in sizes that bracket my own. No time for gold for my toes, I hasten back to the gold for my finger and arrive to find the ring already there. My watch indicates that I finished my tea eight minutes ago.

The jeweler slides the ring onto my finger. It has been polished and there is no trace of the jagged cut. My delight apparent, I begin, "And how much do I—." But the man waves me off.

"You'll be late for your rendezvous."

"Oh, but something, I must pay you something for such excellent service."

"It is nothing."

"No, it is something," I counter. "Please give me some of your cards—for my friends, that they might come to you, too. He does, and I hand him a twenty-lira bill, which we both know can buy virtually nothing at all in inflation-riddled Turkey, not even a glass of tea. "For luck," I explain, "I must leave you something."

He grins, understanding. We shake hands.

"I'll be back," I promise.

"*İnşallah.*"

Granted entry to yet another cell of the city's honeycomb, I feel that much less a stranger—and in my new-found affinity for glitter, ever more an Oriental. I leave to rejoin my companions. My spirit is as burnished as the ring.

> **"Temptations to expense surrounded me everywhere, and I began to think that there was something worth living for in this world."**
>
> **—upon visiting Constantinople and its bazaars**
> ***Hajji Baba of Ispahan* by James Morier, 1824**

Of all things Turkish, only the Topkapı Palace, with its intrigues and sultanic splendor, can match the legendary fame of the *Kapalı Çarşı*, the Covered Bazaar. Since the Turkish conquest of Constantinople, scarcely a literate visitor—Muslim or infidel, novelist or sender of postcards—has not written of the vast marketplace and its wares. Along with the Pyramids, Taj Mahal, Eiffel Tower, and

Disneyland, it continues to occupy a place on the list of world-wonders.

If they think about it at all, few tourists of the last eight or nine years would suppose that the churning activity of the Covered Bazaar could ever have subsided since it was built by order of Mehmet the Conqueror in the middle of the fifteenth century. Any outsider carried through this maze by a Saturday morning crowd would find it impossible to imagine the Bazaar without surging tides of buyers, sellers, and browsers. Though it has known terrible fires, its walls and domes have always risen again to shelter changing inventories. Antimony and bolts of gauze veiling have yielded to Elizabeth Arden cosmetics, blue jeans, and T-shirts. But the spirit of place is unimpaired, and countless treasures await keen eyes and ample purses. What the tourists don't know is that their own growing numbers have helped revitalize a bazaar that in recent years had many vacant stalls.

The first three quarters of the twentieth century did little to foster Turkey's aesthetic development. As the government, educational system, and economy were overhauled, Turkish lifestyles were radically altered. In the name of progress (and much of it was indisputably that), what passed for practicality effected the drabification of Turkey. Istanbul, with its bazaars (Kapalı Çarşı, though the city's greatest, is only one of its many markets) was hard-hit because it had so much to lose. Lightweight aluminum cookware replaced the handsome heavy copper pots that required periodic tinning. Broadloom carpet became cheaper than hand-knotted rugs. And ready-to-wear clothing changed the way everyone looked as colorful regional costumes were superseded by the least-inspired of Western garb. Fez-makers found themselves out of work when men adopted the grey and brown caps of Welsh coal-miners. Girls, unveiled and wearing uniforms, were required to go to school. Craftsmen and household servants left to work in factories; the traditional arts declined as fewer people learned the skills of coppersmithing, silk weaving, gold embroidery.... At the same time, there were fewer hands at home—servants or uneducated sisters—to polish pots and beat rugs. Is it surprising then that housewives developed preferences for Pyrex and linoleum or that young people with French lycée educations wanted overstuffed chairs and dining room suites instead of divans and cushions?

But before it was too late came the reaction and a flash of commercial shrewdness that slowed the rise of mediocrity. Not only did the intelligentsia become interested in their own artistic past, but someone at the Ministry of Tourism awoke to the fact that its campaigns were badly out of focus. (In the early seventies, one infamous travel poster featured a mass of pale, overfed sunbathers on a concrete slab jutting into the Bosphorus. I recall another of a greased wrestling match. A venerable sport in Asia, among foreigners, its appreciation represents a decidedly advanced case of Turcophilia.) Eventually, enlightened functionaries hired top photographers to shoot craggy coastlines, romantically overgrown ruins, and prettily costumed girls taking tea in Ottoman pavilions. This new tack in public relations coincided with the period when the number of Turks working abroad was cresting. Although relations between Turks and the northern Europeans employing them were not always cordial, the mutual acquaintance was irreversible. In short, Turks came home to install porcelain plumbing fixtures and adventurous Westerners who already had a taste for baklava, put aside their notions of the "Terrible Turks," and headed East. And because the new visitors came looking for what was traditionally Turkish, the market was inspired to oblige them. More than anything else, tourism saved Turkish craftsmanship—and the bazaars that sell it—from decay.

Today Western Europeans shop for fabled Oriental souvenirs while Arabs, Hungarians, and Slavs stock up on the modern factory-made goods expensive or unavailable in their home countries. Turks, too, on summer holidays with their *gastarbeiter* wages, have contributed to the prosperity of the Bazaar. A decade ago they wanted the accoutrements of German bathrooms, now they've developed a taste for their own pottery and tribal weavings. New shops have opened in musty stalls long closed, and the powers that be have overseen the repainting of the Bazaar's vaulted passageways. Scaffolding is moved from one section to another as whitewashers and arabesque painters attack mildewed concrete.

While it's undeniable that the Bazaar's offerings include a lot of kitsch, (my favorite examples are the minaret-shaped cologne bottles with attached thermometers), hasn't every age produced its harmless horrors? It is heartening to see fewer dull beige and olive carpets (what a waste of weavers' hours!), and far more village rugs whose hand-spun wools owe their rich palette to the resurgent use of natural dyes.

✱

At dusk the sweepers' brooms push shredded carbons, newspaper, sunflower seed shells, fruit peels, cigarette butts, and cat-sized puffs of rug lint into mounds to be carted off. Porters set down their burdens. Buckets in hand, shopkeepers wash down their thresholds. The cloth sellers refurl their fabrics and bolt wooden shutters. Before they bring screeching steel grates crashing down, the jewelers pull the diamonds from their windows, pack their pearls in flannel, and count their take in global currencies. The gold street goes dark. For the first time since morning, the stream of humanity at the Nuruosmaniye Gate flows in one direction only: out, into the night.

French, German, English, Italian, Greek, Serbo-Croatian, Japanese, Turkish, Persian, Kurdish, Arabic, Ladino...even after hours, the labyrinth echoes with the tongues of its trade. *Kapalı Çarşı* endures.

8

Creature Comforts

DOGS

"If a dog's prayers were answered, bones would rain from the sky."

—Turkish proverb

Like pet dogs themselves, "KÖPEK VAR" signs are still exceptions. While the French warn that their *chiens* are *méchants* and we say "beware," the Turk merely states: "A dog exists." And that is more than enough to deter cat burglars or ne'er-do-well third cousins. The canine advertised may be a teething Spaniel puppy or a chained and snarling German Shepherd; it makes little difference when the average Muslim Turk cares as much for dogs as he does for swine, and fears the species he shuns. On balance, it must be said that many wealthy urban ladies keep miniature French poodles, but they are scarcely considered dogs. Rather, they are play-things or fashion accessories like the knock-offs of Gucci and Louis Vuitton leather goods in Istanbul shops. In a society that remembers, however dimly, times when its people and livestock have lacked sufficient food, it is unsurprising that housepets are not popular.

Until recently, warm-blooded animals have been raised either to be productive or to be eaten. Meryem has always been able to justify her little lamb, but lapdogs are still anomalous luxuries.

But in Turkey, as elsewhere, there is a glaring exception to every tidy generalization.

The original settlers of Polonezköy, the "Polish village" outside Istanbul, were Christian Poles. Though their community shrinks each time another Tadeusz or Barbara leaves to marry an almond-eyed Hulya or mustachioed Mahmut, the hamlet still has a strong Slavic cast. Sloping roofs are bordered with gingerbread, and fat hogs are raised by Christians. And while no Polonezköy Muslim partakes of pork *keilbasa*, both Muslim and infidel keep hunting hounds who seem to spend most of their time asleep. Perhaps they dream of quail season, but the dogs' languor and sagging hides belie any inclination towards blood sports. Having seen their lanky bodies sprawled beneath the plane trees and shop awnings of the village square, one understands why, in cherry season, the owner of a local orchard posts a sign that warns of guardians more intimidating. Nailed to a tree, his hand-lettered board declares:

"There are snakes"

Meanwhile on the Anatolian Plateau, sheepdogs guard the measure of their masters' worth: flocks of fat-tailed sheep whose weighty tails hang lugubriously between their boney legs. Matted fleeces splotched with orange, turquoise, or cerise dyes to distinguish members of different flocks, the herds are an unlikely source of gaiety on this land that has little color except for a few weeks of green wheat and spring wildflowers. The dogs themselves have short, dense coats the color of ripe grain. Related to mastiffs, they are handsome animals who may grow as large as Great Danes. They have floppy ears, heavy jaws, and the powerful limbs of tireless runners. Curling plumes of silky fur, their tails are the Creator's only concession to frivolity. Many of the dogs wear iron collars of medieval design. Studded with sinister two-inch spikes, they protect the dogs when they must defend the herds against wolves.

A creature of narrow loyalty—to his master and the defenseless flock—a Turkish sheepdog is a formidable ally. Or adversary. This and other qualities of the breed are best appreciated from a safe distance. Travellers attracted by the poetry of a shepherd, his dog, and new lambs gambolling against a vernal landscape may be tempted to advance with their cameras. The felt-cloaked shepherd smiles expansively, welcoming your company, and the lambs are docile. But unless the shepherd has a firm grip on his dog's collar, photograph from afar.

"*İt ürür, kervan yürür.*" Onomatopoeic, and growling good advice in fields besides photography: "Dogs bark, but the caravan moves on."

It's a wonder that the main food of these dogs is stale bread. Mutton may well be the staple meat of Turkey, but shepherds themselves eat meat only a few times each year, usually for celebrations.

Providing lambs and wool to sell in the towns, giving milk for yogurt and cheese, sheep are too precious to slaughter for frequent fare. Thus, a sheepdog has few bones to gnaw. (In a telling, Turkish version of the proverb, a dog does not bite the hand that feeds him *bread.*) Yet even the runt of a litter may flourish. I know a gentleman farmer whose weekend retreat supports half a dozen sheep and one healthy, unthreatening, midget sheepdog—a female fancifully named Mercan, which means "coral." "As a puppy, she never got enough to eat," my friend explained. "After her mother's milk, all she had was old bread." Ruefully, he concluded, "Remember we're an underdeveloped country."

But one with superior bread.

CATS

It is said that the Prophet Muhammad
cut off the sleeve of his robe
rather than disturb the cat sleeping upon it.

Calling "Kitty, kitty, kitty!" will not summon one, though with *kedi* being the Turkish word for cat, one would think it might. Instead, cats respond to "psssss, pssss, pssss!" harsh password to the mysterious Eastern feline psyche.

Generally wary of dogs, Turks tolerate cats in the extreme. Less likely to be habitués of the salon than vagrants, cats prowl alleys, wharves, butcher shops, and all but the most snobbish restaurants. Wiley and independent, their notched ears testimony to many a moonlight tussle, most look as if their endless hunt for food were not entirely successful. Their scrawniness and familiarity with trash bins render few of them cuddly.

Of course there are exceptions, and the geographical distribution of cats in Ankara offers a textbook example of urban social stratification. Just proceed through the neighborhoods along Atatürk Boulevard: start from working-class Cebeci, where the winter smog settles, and go up the slope via middle-class Küçükesat, before ascending Çankaya hill, whose magnificent views belong to the diplomatic corps and the wealthiest Turks. The cats mirror their environments. At the bottom of the hill, the gaunt ones with crooked tails, lame limbs, and crossed eyes scramble to eat what little is thrown out and what cannot run away fast enough. Wearing a bit more flesh, the mid-slope cats frequent groceries and restaurants where patrons toss them occasional fish heads and chicken bones. (The sensation of warm fur brushing against one's legs is part of seafood dining here.) At the top of the hill, the fattest cats are solicitously fed by soft-hearted foreigners and indulgent janitors of luxury apartment buildings. While the Cebeci mousers, wary of any human overtures, slink furtively through the shadows, the cats of Çankaya, sunning themselves or taking leisurely baths, feign indifference as they await their tidbit-bearing benefactors.

One family in this neighborhood nourished their adopted street tabby to obesity. The American family fed him twice, but in the tradition of Turkish generosity, their cook and maid each gave him a meal as well. Corpulent and pampered as a pasha, this indolent animal saved his energy to perform one useful service. He killed cockroaches. Though he did not find insects sufficiently dainty for his palate, he liked them well enough for sport. With the cool precision of a hockey player, he would bat them across the kitchen floor until they lay senseless.

Ankara, Ancyra, Angora. The city gave its name not only to Anatolian goats with fine, long-staple wool but also to the local cats. Feline-fanciers look for the stocky body, long white fur, and eye colors (one blue, one amber) of the archetypal Angora cat, a breed officially recognized in North America. Never having seen such a creature in Turkey, I have been told that the so-called Angoras are actually from Van, in southeastern Anatolia. And sure enough, in Van pictures of these cats appear in locally printed tourist literature that relates legends of their affinity for water. But these days the swimming cats of Lake Van are nowhere to be seen, and natives there avow that long ago they were all taken to Ankara. Or to cat shows in Miami Beach?

Ever-observant Evliya Çelebi writes that "in the lands of the Rum, the Arabs, and the Persians there are no cats like those of Divriği, which are beautiful, playful and lovable. They hunt and they are generally well behaved. The cats of Egypt, Trabzon and Sinop are also famous, but these cats of Divriği are fat and big and their fur is as good as that of the otter and very colorful. They take these cats as gifts to the *vilayet* [province] of Ardebil in the land of Persia, where market criers carry them on their heads in cages and sell them to the highest bidders. Some of the bankrupt *kadis* [judges] of Divriği are great misers and they have fifty to sixty of these cats killed every year to provide them with fur. The fur has a reddish shade and cannot be distinguished from the famous squirrel fur of the land of Moscow."

Evliya continues, explaining that Ardebil "is famous for its immense numbers of mice, which are destroyers of cloth. Cats are, therefore...dear; some of Divriği fetch the price of a hundred piastres, but they are short-lived like all cats of Ardebil. The criers at the auction call out: 'A good hunting cat, well bred, a good companion, an enemy to rats, which steals not!'"

On the road to Divriği (one of those roads that seems to lead nowhere else) is the hamlet of Kangal, renowned for its purebred sheepdogs. A traveller in the rain, I glimpsed not a single dog as I passed through Kangal. Later under Divriği's brighter skies, though disappointed to see no cats, I was relieved to meet neither rodents nor fur-clad members of the judiciary.

BIRDS

The tourist is the white dove of peace.
—poster seen in a one-room schoolhouse
Eastern Turkey, 1986

In the parks and mosque courtyards, in virtually any weather, stooped men and women sell paper bags of bread crumbs and saucers of grain, food for the pigeons that flock there. Striking a sympathetic cord among those who would never own dogs or cats, birds are dcar to Turks, who, if they have any pets at all, are most likely to keep canaries, finches, pigeons, or doves.

Istanbul's bird market, cluttered with garden paraphernalia, landscaped by flats of primroses, petunias, dianthus, and salvia, lies along the outer wall of the Egyptian Bazaar. In the open stalls selling rakes, trowels, tubers, seeds, clay flowerpots, gold-fish food, ceramic castles for aquariums, miniature turtles, and jars of leeches, one will find the birds in too-small, bell-shaped cages of wire or bent twigs. On warm days, when the cages hang in the sun, twittering and cooing make this market different from the others, which are invariably dominated by strident cries of vendors.

Across the tea garden, which faces the stalls, is a slightly raised walkway where the letter writers peck at keys of antiquated typewriters. One likes to think that there are still those who, though illiterate (or perhaps *because* they are), revere the printed word. Thus, they eschew the telephone in favor of these cross-legged scribes in thick glasses. Most of the clients are elderly, grown up before the enactment of laws making primary schooling compulsory. It's likely, too, that the recipients of these letters are also untutored, but the senders know that everywhere are younger eyes willing and able to read to the ailing elder brother or widow with marriageable daughters back in the village. That such missives are neither written nor read in privacy is unremarkable in a culture that has no word for the condition. It seems particularly appropriate that chattering birds and fishbowls occupy space opposite the letter-writers' station, where any passerby can eavesdrop and read over the typists' shoulders....

For a few cents, the passive pedlar of portents, the *niyetçi* who works this area, will have his pigeon peck (or rabbit nibble) at a tray filled with folded slips of paper:

> **"You shall receive a letter from your heart's desire."**
> **"With patience, mulberry leaves become silk."**

Fortunes without cookies.

But better to find a more-or-less level table in the garden and order tea or an infusion of linden blossoms. The edges of scent and sound become blurred where potting soil, damp burlap, and bird-seed share the air with an avian chorus, clinking tea glasses, and the determined ring of an old Olivetti.

The garden has an atmosphere that encourages contemplation of the past and its sayings. To describe a work of architecture as "a birdcage," is to remark on its beauty and delicacy. How seldom can that compliment be paid to the bad Bauhaus concrete of the modern Levant!

A desolate place is one where "no bird flies and no caravan passes." The polluted air that pits the sidewalks and cement buildings of Turkish cities also stifles the nightingales of the Bosphorus and spares but a few sparrows in Ankara. How do the caged canaries survive? Doubtless, the caravans, with their cargoes of Far Eastern electronics and American cigarettes, will continue to arrive here, even if every wing is stilled. How long before language reflects reality and birds leave the proverb as they've left the cities?

"Bird" is slang for a foolish gambler,
in other words, a "pigeon."

Evliya Çelebi recounts an old-fashioned saying of his father's time (the sixteenth century): "Who kills a bird-merchant or a gambler may be called a warrior for the faith." But a generation later, it is clear many still plied those trades. Pigeon-keeping and betting on bird games are blamed for the financial ruin of young men, who, Evliya notes, even bedeck their birds "with ear and feet-rings."† One amateur of the highly-esteemed Baghdad letterdoves

†This is still done in Turkey, in the area between Gaziantep and Urfa. See the chapter "Journeys: The Southeast"

feeds his beloved birds "with pomegranate grains wrapt in musk."

In the library of the British Museum, lies a tiny Koran with octagonal pages. Its miniature Arabic script, a style called *ghabarah*, meaning "dust," was especially devised for communiqués carried by pigeons. On a wing and a prayer?

In Istanbul, near what was once the French Embassy, are sombre grey stone walls embellished by tiny Ottoman stone "bird pavilions." And elsewhere in the city, old gravestones, with their little basins, still catch rainwater for feathered visitants whose wing-beats and song ease the melancholy of souls yet to make the passage to Paradise.

9

Intermezzo

A LITTLE NIGHT MUSIC

"Such sweet compulsion doth in music lie."

—*Arcades* (1630-34) by John Milton

Tour groups ("...floor show and one cocktail per person...our bus departs at eight-thirty sharp...") fill most of the tables in the nightclubs where the master of ceremonies extends greetings in nine languages and jokes in four. And there's always a sprinkling of businessmen from Des Moines, Dusseldorf, Tokyo.... The orchestra caters to its polyglot audience with abbreviated versions of "Yellow Rose of Texas," "O Tannenbaum," "Lady of Spain," "Arrivederci, Roma," and accordion polkas. Far from their home provinces, adolescent folk troupes—

spoon dancers, bagpipers, and *zeybek*s in striped cummerbunds—step and leap with dour proficiency. Magicians reconstitute the silk scarves they've shredded and pull eggs from behind ears. In their sequins, fringe, chiffon, and finger cymbals, the belly-dancers arrive on the stage to ripple their pale midriffs in solo numbers before they drag tourists, tipsy on *rakı*, into the spotlight. For most of the patrons, this will be their sole night out of the promised Thousand and One. At inflated prices, the ever-present photographer can provide souvenirs of chagrin.

How long has it been since the best bellydancers left for Beirut?

"Before your time," they tell me, "And now they've gone to Athens and London."

He looks like a lot of men—tenderly sad-faced and stooped, with a crooked bow tie and a few strands of hair carefully combed and recombed across a bald spot. Late forties, unmarried and probably living at home with his mother. He is playing an electric organ in the hotel lobby for the welcome cocktail party of my tour group, just-arrived in Ankara. I wince when I hear a little tremolo in "Tie a Yellow Ribbon;" this could be a Ramada Inn in New Jersey! I wish I could persuade him not to serenade us, but it is the first time I've brought a group to this hotel and I don't want to antagonize anyone—yet. But someday I'd like to have a serious discussion with the powers who assume foreigners want to hear abroad what invades their lives at home.

I am relieved that the group, enjoying gin-and-tonics, cherry juice with vodka, and rosé, is paying no discernible attention to "Begin the Beguine." (The organ has those tabs you can push to activate assorted syncopations.) In an idle moment, the drinks waiter drums his fingers on the bar in time to the music. As we, the inattentive audience, leave the lounge to take dinner in the hotel's restaurant, the bartender turns to the organist and says in Turkish, "Hit it, Faik Bey, hit it!" Faik Bey does just that, and we withdraw to strains of "Home on the Range."

Later, as the orders for Turkish coffee are taken and the jet-lagged drift off to their rooms, Faik Bey reappears. He draws the white cover from the baby grand piano, until now unnoticed at one end of the dining room, and plays with a delicate, accomplished touch—Schumann, then Mozart. Astounded, I sit listening; the waiters clear around me. The last tour members, seeimgly as oblivious to this performance as they were to the cocktail tunes, say good-night. They're exhausted, I know, but I wish they'd stay, at least for a few more minutes. I ask myself why a musician who can play like this also cranks out background music in a hotel bar, but I know it's for the same reasons there are competent musicians doing the same thing the world over. Faik Bey lifts his hands from the keys and flips through the sheet music before him. I walk up and tell him, in English, how much I enjoy his playing, especially the Mozart. Somehow it seems more appropriate to compliment him in a foreign language for his mastery of a foreign art. Faik Bey smiles shyly and bends over the keyboard, giving himself again to a little night music.

Every year as part of the Istanbul Summer Festival, two or three performances of Mozart's opera *Abduction from the Seraglio* are given in the Seraglio of Topkapı itself. (*Saray*, Turkish for "palace," is the root of the Italian "*seraglio.*") In the open air of the third courtyard, before the Gate of Felicity, to the right of the Harem and to the left of the emerald-filled Treasury, a stage is set up. With spray-painted plywood panels mimicking a home-made Alhambra, almost all the stage scenery is comically redundant. The real arches, leaded domes, and towers of the sultans surround the audience.

A fine little orchestra plays beneath a giant *çınar* tree, its leaves stirred by Mozart's overture, complete with the jingling Turkish bells and cymbals that beguiled eighteenth-century Europe. As a safety precaution and display of municipal might, a fire engine has been parked between the Gate of the Birdcage and the chamber housing the Mantle of the Prophet. We five foreign women, on folding metal chairs in the front row of the audience, are still reeling in wonder at our good fortune. Only fifteen minutes ago, we were buying tickets to a sold-out performance from a scalper in the shadows of the Gate of Salutations.

There is no printed program, so we have no inkling as to the names or nationalities of the principals, who sing their arias in Mozart's original German. I speculate whether all the spoken lines of the slapstick wine-drinking scene will be left intact, and am not surprised the reference to "Mahomet" is deleted. Why risk offending any fundamentalist opera buffs?

It has rained just before the performance, and Istanbul is notorious for its shower-induced power outages. Well into the opera, towards the end of one lively scene, the stage suddenly goes dark. Someone switches on the headlights of the fire-engine, but their illumination falls short of the stage, where the four lovers are valiantly continuing their quartet in total obscurity. One of our companions pulls a focussing pocket flashlight from her purse and trains its beam on the singers. Amidst an outbreak of applause, the singers deliver their final notes before the flashlight beam guides them back-stage.

The electricity restored, the opera proceeds smoothly to its joyous finale. As live white doves are released into the moonlit night, the chorus of full-voiced extras sings rousingly—not in German, but in Turkish! "Long live the Pasha!"

10

A Few of the Men

**"You'll never plumb the Oriental mind,
And if you did it isn't worth the toil."**

**—*Departmental Ditties, One Viceroy Resigns*,
by Rudyard Kipling, 1886**

RASİM

Istanbul-born, blond Rasim, with Thracian blood and an Arab name, has no problem considering himself a New Yorker after eight years in the city. However, he says he intends to remain a Turk. Reading the American edition of the Turkish newspaper *Hürriyet* (Independence) and New York's *Daily News*, he'll lunch on a tuna fish sandwich from the corner deli (Greek-run, not too bad). But he still mistrusts even all-beef hot dogs (the threat of pork) and fears the blacks who ride the subways with him from Queens will tail him and rob his rug shop on the third floor of a building on 29th Street. He worries about his alarm system, a receding hairline, and the health of his parents back in Istanbul. Were he in Turkey, he'd be even more preoccupied with them, and his mother would try to fatten him up. He wouldn't be making as much money (God knows he wouldn't need an alarm), but he'd still be going bald.

Rasim met his pretty Mexican wife when she was a bilingual secretary in London. She's learned Turkish and can stuff a grape leaf as well as a tamale. Now that she's the mother of his two sons, he doesn't want her to work outside the house. The boys are called Attila and Cengiz. Noble, heroic names...for Turks. To myself, I say, "Just wait 'til those kids start school in Queens...."

HİDAYET

Years ago when I first saw them together, I didn't know which was more extraordinary, Hidayet Efendi or the yard-long carrots he carried like an armload of firewood. But later whenever I encountered those enormous red winter carrots that invariably called him to mind, I realized Hidayet Efendi was the more remarkable. And Hidayet, with the ashy circles beneath his blood-shot eyes and a voice that made basso profundo sound like a canary's twitter, suggested things far deeper than root crops. Initially, I found him terrifying—his low Anatolian hairline with its wolfish widow's peak, the shelf of eyebrow, the tobacco-colored skin, the dusty clothing. Yet there was nothing ugly about him, no deformity. He smoked noxious cigarettes, and his gruff speech was punctuated by horrible coughing that rose from unknown depths. By all appearances a Turkish incarnation of Vulcan, he was simply an old family retainer almost beyond the age of usefulness.

Kenan and Turhan had him do simple chores at the farm or sent him shopping for items like carrots, which required little discernment. In the country manner, we always left our shoes at the door before entering the house. When mud was in season, it was Hidayet who saw that our boots were brushed clean before we put them on again. He fed and watered Lisa, the mongrel poodle, who, like outdoor footwear, was not allowed into the house. But at night she shared Hidayet's spare little room in a side building. Lisa and he, each with more bark than bite, were the only guardians of the farm. Hidayet's most important function was as a presence. His voice alone could repulse any trespasser, be he vandal or fruit-thief. Yet once one was used to him, he seemed the soul of gentleness.

When she made *mantı* with lots of garlicked yogurt and melted butter, Turhan would call him in to lunch with the women and children. Like a tamed bear dressed and capable of going through the motions of human activity, he sat at the table with us and ate quickly, a huge spoon and a chunk of bread his preferred utensils. Turhan, her plump, jewelled hand ladelling out bowls of the hot pasta, would encourage his appetite. "*Al, Hidayet Efendi, biraz daha al*! Take it, take some more!"

"Turhan *Abla*..., Turhan my sister," he would growl appreciatively. The tenderness of their address, like the sacred act of sharing a meal, transcended their social disparities. Neither would have wished to trade places with the other, just as neither feared the fortunes foretold by the dregs of the coffee they took after lunch.

When Hidayet died from cigarettes and Allah-alone-knows-what-else, Kenan pursued the rumors that he had left a son. Though a bachelor almost all his life, Hidayet had married a girl who had abandoned him and their young son when she ran off with her lover. The boy grew up in another home and had little contact with his father. Kenan managed to trace the young man to a village not far from Konya. The boy had yet to marry, and without family or wealth, his chances for making a match for himself were severely impaired. Kenan says succintly, "So, in his father's memory, we gave him a job and found him a wife."

Even in the countryside, where paternalism hangs on, Kenan's bothering to locate the child of a dead servant was beyond what anyone would have expected. But this coda is as much a tribute to the servant as to the master. True charity like Kenan's is not instigated by guilt or pity, it is inspired by respect. Through fidelty to those who were not even kin, Hidayet unwittingly provided a legacy of dignity to a son who scarcely knew him.

When people here speak of honor, it is a steely ideal, the sort that too often has led to debate at sword-point. The concept usually embodies heroics of illustrious ancestors and protection of female virtue. With these attributes conspicuously absent from the narrative, Hidayet's son's windfall of good luck is just short of miraculous. Hidayet, who possessed little more than his honorific *efendi*, managed to leave an estate.

Kenan was the executor.

GAZİ

Whenever there is a hard rain, as there has been tonight, the electricity fails in Polonezköy. The driveway is dark as we roll through the gate, past the Dobermans straining on their chains, and down to the garage. Kenan leaves the headlights on until Gazi, lamp in hand, hurries out to us.

From the front seat of the car, Kenan grabs his canvas pouch containing a few business papers, several pipes, and some tobacco. He is about to sling it over his shoulder, but Gazi reaches to take it. We cross the wet flagstones bordering the dripping shrubbery and enter the house through the kitchen, where Kenan lights a kerosene lamp. Hissing, it brings the room to life.

"How long has the power been off?" asks Kenan.

"Only half an hour. We've had no problems," answers Gazi.

From the refrigerator, I remove the thawing turbot steaks we were to have fixed for our dinner.

Since we ate two hours ago in Istanbul and shall be out tomorrow night as well, I ask, "Gazi, do you like fish? *Kalkan*? Have you had supper yet?" He smiles shyly, his face lit by the hand lantern.

"Thank you. No, not this evening." Kenan raises his eyebrows. The country people go to bed at dark, yet Gazi here, has not even had his supper though it is past ten.

"You know how to cook *kalkan*?" He nods and looks at me in a polite way that makes me suspect he does not. He is from Konya, inland, where fish is seldom eaten. "I like to fry it in a little oil—or butter," I say, remembering that the latter is what Konyans would use. "No more than four or five minutes on a side. Then I squeeze some lemon on it. Really delicious." Along with a lemon from the fruit bin, I hand him the platter of fish. "Here, and *Afiyet olsun*! May there be plenty!"

"Thank you again. Good night." He is beaming, and probably very hungry, as he backs out the door into the night.

"I'm surprised he hasn't eaten."

"His wife's a funny woman, not exactly lazy, but she doesn't do a lot of the things that one would expect," says Kenan.

"Like cook?"

"Well, yes. We found her, you know, as a bride for Gazi, and we built them their house out by the gate." I think of the white-washed stucco cottage with the red hollyhocks and sleeping dogs in the yard. "And she's never invited us inside, not even at Bayram. She's the daughter of a *hoca*, very conservative. We thought she'd make a good wife, but... they have no children.... People gossip and say, well, you know the sort of things they would say around here. Who knows? Maybe what they say is true. But it's a shame. He's a good man."

A good man. I remember the afternoon when Gazi was hosing down the rose beds and pittosporum and I was idly pinching off yellowed geranium leaves. He looked up from his work, noticed me, and I saw his look of bewildered embarrassment. I was performing a task that was rightfully his; I should not have strayed into his realm—garden maintenance. In particular, I should not have done something that had probably never even occurred to him. For a moment, I had caused him to loose face before me, a guest of the house.

Sweet Gazi. He alone can talk to the dogs, calm them, make them lick his hands. They would tear anyone else to shreds. (Hadn't they nearly gotten Kenan's brother-in-law last summer? Kenan keeps them to deter burglars, but they also deter visitors. I find them terrifying.) But Gazi can play with them as if they were kittens.

He cares for the horses, the sheep, and the cow as well. When he brings Turhan warm milk from the barn, she makes it into yogurt with a thick skin on top and always gives some to him.

One hot afternoon during Ramazan I was wearing a bathing suit as I sunned on the terrace. Not more than thirty meters away, Gazi and another laborer were scything hay in a field. I could barely hear their voices. They were part of the background sounds of the day—the breeze rustling the leaves of the nearby woodland, the mockingbirds, the swish of the scythe through the dry grass, the bees humming in the roses. I was dozing when Turhan appeared and suggested I put on something less revealing. "It's not fair to Gazi and his friend," she said, "especially when they must fast and think only pure thoughts."

Often during that holy month, Turhan would prepare *börek* in a large tray. After sundown she would take half of it to Gazi and reserve the rest for her family. He would have it for supper and again before dawn, to fortify himself for a new day of self-denial.

Until tonight, I've never known about Gazi's withdrawn wife or, indeed, anything more about him than what is strung on this short thread of recollection. A good man, the sort that comes to mind when someone says "salt of the earth." He deserves a fine dinner. I hope he enjoys the fish.

11

Other Than Odalisques

GOLDEN SHOES

We're outdoors, and a dusky Kurdish woman wearing a gold stud in one nostril, a white, bead-trimmed headscarf, and full skirts sits weaving a wool kilim on a simple loom. Standing around her is our band of tourists, rug-fanciers watching and photographing. A younger woman in Western dress kneels down to join the first weaver at her work. She is fair, with dyed coppery hair falling to her shoulders. I notice her chipped red fingernail polish when she strums the warp yarns on the loom. On her feet are incongruous gold high-heeled sandals.

"Is she a local woman?" I ask Farid, who has brought us to this village to see the weaving.

"Excuse me, which woman?" he asks.

"The redhead in the golden shoes," I say, but Farid does not answer. "I mean, does she live here, in this village, or is she from outside? A visitor? A teacher?"

"She's local," Farid whispers, closing his eyes, as if submitting to something unpleasant. He seems unhappy with my interest in the woman who seems as foreign in this settlement as the tourists.

Presently Golden Shoes, clutching a handbag, leaves her place at the loom and departs. We linger a short while as Farid, a Kurd himself, translates the group's questions for the weaver and her answers. The village is participating in a very successful rural development project that enables women to learn weaving so they may supplement their family incomes. Farid is as proud of the women's efforts as he is of his own, for he is the project coordinator.

We board our bus for the fifteen-minute ride back to our hotel in the town. Where the village lane meets the asphalt highway, someone stands waiting for a *dolmuş*. About to regain the highway, we see that it is Golden Shoes. More than one American voice calls out that we should give her a lift into town. We stop and she hops on, taking the empty front seat beside me.

We chat, posing the usual questions. "You are from Istanbul?" she asks. She could as easily say "Mars." This is eastern Anatolia and her Turkish is rough, throaty, familiar. My polite second-person plural is a city mannerism, almost an affectation out in the country. And since Kurdish is her first language, she doesn't readily recognize my own accent in Turkish. Here, I'm foreign in any sense, any language. Especially in Turkish. I am not *yerli*, literally not "of this place," and she knows it.

"No, I'm American."

"But you know Turkish! What language do you speak with these people?"

"English."

"Ahh, nice." She smiles and asks if I am married. When I say yes, she asks if one of the male members of the group is my husband.

"No, I'm here alone—working, showing Turkey to tourists." Accustomed to the outpouring of astonished commentary this admission of independence can provoke, especially in Turkey, I try to steer the conversation back to her. She wears a wedding ring, so I say, "You're married, what does your husband do?"

"He's a worker at the government tree farm near the airport." I'm about to ask about her children when she leans forward to tell our bus driver to drop her just ahead, at a particular corner in the town. For the next minute we smile at each other and exchange the pleasantries of farewell. "Go laughingly," I say.

"*Allaha ismarladık.* I have commended you to God," she answers. "Have a nice trip." We shake hands before her glittering feet step purposefully into the stream of pedestrians. From the sidewalk, she waves to all of us.

Later, Farid feels obligated to enlighten us and reveals that Golden Shoes, like the village weavers, also contributes to her household's earnings. According to him, we in our innocent charity, the charity of travellers to one another, have delivered a woman of easy virtue to her clients.

SEMAHAT

From the beach, it looks like Gibraltar. Except that this is the wrong end of the Mediterranean. Far across the sea lies the Sinai, not the Maghreb. The headland of Alanya is crowned by a ruined Selcuk fortress enclosing remains of an early Christian church, but the spectacle here is more topographical than architectural. Alaettin Keykubat's thirteenth-century stone defenses, like so many of the ruins in this country, evoke a history romantically vague rather than insistently specific.

I prefer a place like this, whose original significance is blurred by centuries of surrounding settlement, to a more famous monument, well-kept and kept apart. Today sheep graze inside the walls, while goats browsing for weeds in the creviced masonry negotiate crumbling ramparts. It is peaceful here, with only the wind sighing in the wild grasses and the voices of girls trying to sell crochet-edged headscarves to scatterings of tourists. In clear weather the sea, a hundred yards below, shimmers turquoise, violet, green. One can gaze both east and west along the pale beaches. The scarf girls draw me aside to ask if I have medicine for one of them who has a stomachache. I don't, so they wander off, except for one who watches me, yet another foreigner examining wildflowers.

I find an intensely aromatic plant, nearly a yard tall with small greyish leaves and tight round flower buds. I pick a few sprigs, and then the girl joins in, handing me what she gathers. "In winter we brew it like tea," she says. "We also boil it to collect the oil from the leaves, to make a salve that is good for cuts and burns." I ask her the name of the plant and am not surprised when she answers *kekik*, meaning marjoram and oregano, as well as thyme. (The common Turkish names for plants are maddeningly imprecise. To most Turks any blossom not a rose is either a "daisy" or, merely, a "flower." I deem this particular plant oregano.) The girl asks about the man who has accompanied me, my husband. "Is he a professor?" I laugh, congratulating her for recognizing the distinctive markings of the species—sturdy walking shoes and a notebook. Together within the fortress, we collect an armful of oregano. My husband takes a photograph of us, each with an arm around the other's waist. Twelve years old, her name is Semahat, and she carefully writes her mailing address (in care of her father, a mechanic at the Alanya municipal garage) so that we may send her a copy of the picture. She gives me a maroon scarf, elaborately edged with loops and tiny white beads. We pay for another—a gift for the girl watering our house plants back in New England.

Five years later, almost to the day, I return to the Alanya Castle, where a group of girls still sells scarves at the gate. Semahat is not among them. Perhaps she has outgrown the activity, maybe she's married. I ask the girls if they know her, and they chatter excitedly among themselves before one scurries down to the village below. "If she comes," I tell them and gesture, "I am over there, picking *kekik.*" Hoping to replenish my kitchen herb supply, I am disappointed when I find just a few plants. Not wanting to decimate the patch, I break off only a few sprigs before the girls call me. I turn back towards them and pretty Semahat is in their midst. She doesn't remember me, at first.

I remind her about the photograph, say I still have the headscarf and her father's address at the garage. Did she ever receive the photo I mailed? Yes, she begins to recollect. And the *kekik*, doesn't she remember that? She nods slowly.

Tentatively, she asks, "You were with your husband, a professor? But how did you remember me for all those years?"

"How could I forgot you? Every time I cook with *kekik* I think of you! And it has not been so long, only five years." But to someone seventeen... I suppose five years is a long time. Adhering to the rituals of reacquaintance, I inquire about the well-being of her family, even though I've never met them. She tells me her older sister will marry within the month. "And you? You're still in school?"

"I've finished at the lycée, and I had really wanted to go on to the university, but, well...I studied hard for the test, but my score was one point too low. Only one point...and they wouldn't pass me. I couldn't believe it!" She sighs. "I might go to work at the bank here in Alanya. I like to meet people—foreigners. I want to practice my English."

"You could practice it right now," I say, switching into English, "with me." But she blushes and remains silent, until I return to Turkish. "What has happened to the *kekik*? It seems to have died out."

"No. I'll show you where to look." And Semahat leads me through the ruins to a vigorous spread of the silvery green herb, more pungent here than anywhere else in Turkey. We gather masses of it and a tourist snaps our picture. This time, it is I who ask for a copy of the photo.

And four years after that I'm back again. The scarf-sellers remind me which of the hill-sided houses belongs to her family. As I approach, ascending the steep, geranium-lined walk, I call up, asking a plump young woman crocheting if Semahat is home. Another girl, slight and scarved in white, comes racing down the path. It is Semahat, and we joyfully embrace. She leads me by the hand to her terrace where her sister, brother-in-law, parents, and grandmother sit on this warm afternoon. "Mother, we need tea!" says Semahat, like a chatelaine, proprietary in her possession of me, the exotic. And her mother, who has already kissed my cheeks, cheerfully disappears to brew tea, despite my protests. It is Ramazan, so I know the family is fasting; they will sit watching me sip what they must forego. Of course, my protest is to no avail. A guest, any guest, conveys honor and must be served refreshment.

Semahat wears tiny gold earrings and a ring, investments of what she's earned crocheting. Alanya has more tourists now and the scarf business is good. Even when she's not peddling her handiwork, she's able to spend her time outdoors crocheting and breathing the breeze from the sea. At twenty-one, she earns more on her own than if she worked for the bank. And she has time for a German pen-pal whose Turkish letters she corrects....

Prosperity: the stone house has just been whitewashed; a television prattles on in the empty sitting room. Here on the terrace, the family hangs on the words of their unmarried girl and her guest. I take tea as they quench their thirst with our conversation. Semahat smiles upon the plastic sack beside my feet. The scent gives it away. "*Kekik*," we say in tandem.

High above the streets in the towns one sees the peasant maids washing apartment windows. Scarved and ruddy-cheeked, they work in fearless pursuit of dulling dirt and detergent streaks. Stocky Fatma or Remsiye is steadied by a genetically low center of gravity and one bloomered leg planted inside the window frame.

Historically, foreign visitors to the Levant were wont to complain of the untidiness, if not filth, of its cities. But rarely has that criticism ever crossed the threshhold of a Turkish house inhabited by a least one woman. If the swept, scrubbed, and polished interiors of even the poorest homes have floors clean enough to eat from, it's because for centuries Turks have done just that. Traditional dwellings had little wooden furniture and life was lived below the windowsill, among cushions and rugs. In rural areas, meals are still taken from a communal tray set on the floor.

The efficient and cheerful industry of Turkish housekeepers is one of the luxuries residents, especially foreign residents, have long enjoyed. Unfortunately, unlike dried apricots and fine carpets, servants are not, except in rare instances, a Turkish commodity exported to North America.

Even if one did not already know it as the most architecturally flamboyant of Washington's Beaux Arts embassies, one would surely guess the address of the Turkish legation by the periodic appearance of a calico-clad caryatid on its upper cornices.

At the other end of the social spectrum is Billur, sixtyish *grande dame* brandishing a silver-headed cane on which I have not noticed her lean. "It clears people out of the way," she explains as she cuts a swath through an airport crowd. She grew up in her family's sprawling 52-room *yalı* on the European side of the Bosphorus. "You can't begin to imagine," she says, "what life for a child was like in that hothouse—surrounded by three generations of relatives, all those cousins, unmarried aunts and uncles. Such intrigues, a real school for scandal. My grandmother used to say of the place: 'Come in the morning as a virgin and you'll leave that evening as a widow.'"

And Gabriella, in the sales deparment of one of Istanbul's five-star hotels. She is a *tatlı su ferengi*, a "Sweet-Water foreigner," as the Istanbul-born Europeans are called, after the cool springs in Galata, their enclave. Tracing their families back centuries, to the time of the Ottoman capitulations to Western traders, Gabriella's parents are German and Italian. I deduce that she must speak five languages: Turkish, German, Italian, French (even now the lingua franca of Levantine Christians and Jews), and English (the language of hotel telexes). She smiles, her perfect teeth glistening. With matter-of-fact charm she says, "Six, actually."

"And the sixth is...?"

"Greek." Of course, the speech of the Second Rome. One must not forget that this is still Byzantium.

TURKISH TAPESTRY

"Wine loved I deeply, dice dearly, and in women out-paramoured the Turk."

—William Shakespeare (Edgar in *King Lear* Act III, Scene IV)

I've known scores of them—former Peace Corps volunteers, left-over hippies, minor art history majors, secretaries of multinational corporations, bored wives of boring diplomats, fugitives, footloose romantics, and professional dilettantes. Each one somehow enlightened, ensnared, enthralled by the East, they are among the women drawn to (or washed up on?) what Lesley Blanche charted as "the wilder shores of love."

All of them have lost their hearts to Turkey, and some have had theirs stolen by Turks. Their stories are as vivid and poignant as the miniature paintings in the precious manuscripts displayed under dim lights in the museums. Despite the sumptuous pigments and gilding, those worlds—of Aslı, Layla, and Shirin, the heroines of the great Middle Eastern epics—remain two-dimensional, morally black and white. Through painstaking detail, the miniatures illustrate realms of appealing simplicity where everyone understands what is permitted—and forbidden. It is only on the grey slate of our modern age that choices are possible and necessary. Still, what is discretionary in Paris is better kept discreet in Istanbul. Dogs bark, but when the reputation of a woman is an issue, the caravan does not move on—it stalls. Both camels and pilgrims will crane their necks for a better view.

It's only natural that one should wonder, especially since she has occupied herself with this culture for so long.... The society seduced her some time ago, but what about *one of them*?

Or was it that *she* found some quarry amongst that thicket of moustaches? Interesting questions, and not at all irrelevant, even if they are prurient. She doesn't mind (much) that you inquire, but she's not sure how she'll answer.

The very success of her assimilation distances her from the other expatriates, yet she has far more in common with them than she likes to contemplate. She knows their shallowness firsthand, and fearing the same in herself, draws away from the ladies' luncheons and the places her people gather. She is lonely, but then, she was that before she ever came to Turkey, where even the forlorn rarely know solitude. Here, privacy is so foreign a concept it lacks a name.

She is an enigma to the Turks, most of whom cannot comprehend her devotion to Oriental aspects of a society they wish were more "European." More than her appearance, it is usually her Turkish, far from perfect but bordering on the colloquial, that allows her (if she wears a headscarf) to blend into the crowd. Fascinated by the idea of a complete union with the place and wondering how to consummate it, she considers the possibility of a Turkish lover, a mate for both spirit and body. But this is mentioned to no one. Even to herself she never says "taking" a lover, though that would reinforce the image of herself she likes best: mistress of her own destiny.

She has been training the tendrils of Orientalism long enough to have entangled herself in the overgrown garden of paradox. Willing to trust such things as *muhabbet* (loving affection) to *kısmet* (fate), she indulges in the perilous fantasy that these abstractions cannot be translated. Quite simply, she feels that being "in control" of her heart would drain any affair, and most surely a Turkish one, of all romance. But at the same time, the common sense by which she has so far survived makes her spurn the too-avid attentions bestowed by the legions of Turks who would squire her for nothing more than her fair hair. Enthusiastically seconding her opinion that their culture is superior to anything else she has known, they are enticed less by her appreciation of their heritage than by the status any foreign woman grants her escort. That she might love Turkey but choose to resist the attractions of able-bodied Turks like themsleves is a conundrum they are incapable of discussing or even imagining. (The obstacles to enduring relationships are rarely linguistic, for their English is almost always better than her Turkish.)

She is loathe to generalize, but experience leads her to conclude that the majority of Turkish men cannot fathom why any woman would wish to be loved for her mind. (What a terrible thing to say, she thinks.) When the other foreign women gossip about "the unbridled lust" of Turks, she remains silent, embarrassed to admit any agreement. In truth, she'd like to defend the men, to supply an unemotional, socio-ethnological explanation for their molten stares and swagger. Unfortunately, she knows better. Needless to say, when our heroine falls for someone she thinks is an exception, she falls very hard indeed....

Her parents were with the American Embassy. She had fishished a year or two of college when she came to visit them in Ankara. I don't know how she met the Turkish boyfriend who was the reason she didn't return to the States when her father's tour of duty finished. To her parents' dismay, the couple rented an apartment in Ankara and were married. He was a salesman and frequently out of town. She taught yoga. I had never heard of them until a friend, an embassy administrative officer, asked me to accompany the girl to the airport and see that she left the country safely and without incident.

The afternoon before she had appeared at the embassy and announced that she was leaving her husband and wanted to return to the States. Her parents had been notified, and much relieved, they wired funds for her return flight. She explained to the officer that she needed to leave as soon as possible. She had not taken much more than the clothes she was wearing, an odd get-up of a cotton turtleneck, calico *şalvar*, and sandals. She had not wanted to alert her husband to her departure, so she had left behind her possessions and had not even written him a note. She still loved him, she said, but he was extremely jealous. He accused her of flirting while he was away, and he had, on occasion, beaten her. If he had any notice of her escape, she knew he would search for her, and she feared he might hurt someone, possibly himself.

The embassy gave us a car and driver for the forty-five minute trip to the airport. For most of the drive she wrote in a round hand on the lined yellow legal pad balanced on her knees. It was a letter to her husband, and I glanced at it from time to time. Considering this dramatic finale, it seemed a dispassionate missive (in a "sorry-the-vibrations-weren't-better" tone). When she had finished, she sealed it in an envelope and asked me to post it after her plane had taken off.

Initially, there must have been some pleasurable passion in their union, and it was clearly passion of another sort that drove her to leave him. But such a pallid parting? What difference might it make if I did not mail the letter? But mail it I did before phoning my friend at the embassy to report that the flight to Washington had just left and that the girl had been on it.

The episode was over, but it had left me uneasy. Though the girl and I were about the same age and had similar coloring, not even the kind of Turk who thinks all Americans look alike could confuse us. Or so I hoped. We were completely different, I told myself and wondered at one damnable coincidence: we shared the same first name!

"La rosa enflorece, En el mez de May, Mi alma s'escurece, Sufriendo del amor.	"The rose flowers, In the month of May, My soul is darkened, Suffering from love.
Los bilbilicos cantan, Sospiran del amor Y la pasion me mata Muchigua mi dolor."	The little nightingales sing, Sighing of love, And passion murders me, So great is my pain."

—Traditional Ladino song of the Turkish Sephardim
Anthology of Sephardic Songs, compiled by Issac Levy

There are those who, having given up on the men, lavish affection on pets, dogs usually. Take the grey-eyed girl with the panting creature straining at his leash. I've heard it said that she's chosen the arthritic mongrel shepherd over all the who men who would woo her. Without the dog, she'd die of loneliness, the way she almost died after she left the Turk she loved because she could no longer bear him criticizing her clothes, her friendliness to the grocer, or a hundred other things, including what he called her "lack of modesty." And she nearly died again when he let his parents arrange his marriage to a macaroni heiress.

Turkish society really has no place for a young woman alone. After her stint in the Istanbul office of XYZ Corporation is completed or her grant money has run out or the dog has expired, she may linger nonetheless. And if she doesn't go home, back to Boston or Johannesburg or Vancouver, it's because after her time away, those places are no longer home. Besides, the Turks will always accord her respect and make allowances for her, an alien, a guest in perpetuity. She is free from political and social responsibilities she would have to shoulder in her native land. Life here requires only that she comport herself with dignity. If nothing wrenches her away, it is so easy to stay on in the little mouse-riddled apartment with the splendid view beyond the minaret, beyond her somewhat faded, though still fashionable, quarter of Istanbul. Just as she once developed a taste for the simultaneously bitter and sweet coffee, she has grown accustomed to the qualified privileges of a life she feels she could sustain nowhere else. Being here becomes an end in itself, and the means by which she remains are diverse. As the Turks say, she has a few "gold bracelets." The allusion is to a woman's dowry jewelry, emblematic of the skills by which she can, if need arise, support herself.

She can always do translations of brochures for tourist facilities and shops; their prose is so awful that it matters little whether her English is faithful to every word in the original Turkish text. But that's depressing, reclusive work with meagre pay. There are other, more enjoyable, ways of making ends meet. Being youngish and fair, she was once asked to model some leather clothing for a manufacturer targetting the German market. And she was a part-time film projectionist for one of the foreign language cinemas. Like an Oriental, she lives from day to day. She tries not to think too much about those expatriate women in their fifties and sixties, who have spent half their lives in niches like hers. There's one who manages to live off the articles she writes for local hotel magazines, and another, a wizened photographer of nomads, who seems to subsist only on unfiltered Black Sea cigarettes.

Having long since ceased pining for the gallant princes of the exquisite illuminations, these older women have struck a precarious bargain with their adopted society. Had they gone back to their own kind, they would have sacrificed the status granted by their years. In the East, age commands respect. During their extended residencies, these women have themselves become players in the very drama at which they were once open-mouthed spectators. There may be few parts for the alien ingénue, but the Turks literally kiss the hands of older eccentrics. Indeed, Islam bids the sane to indulge the mad.

Women, too, have left other shores to follow Yeats in *Sailing to Byzantium*:

> "That is no country for old men. The young
> In one another's arms, birds in the trees
> --Those dying generations..."

And neither is theirs for old women, so each echoes the poet—

> "...And therefore I have sailed the seas and come
> To the holy city of Byzantium..."

Whether she is complacent, timid, plucky, or unendingly curious, something keeps her staying on in Turkey.

It is hard to relinquish a flag of convenience.

12

Taking the Waters

"Water vivifies all things."

—The *Koran*

In all the thirst-inducing footage of *Lawrence of Arabia*, whose lyrical cinematography committed too many compelling clichés to film, a single Turkish word is spoken. A dying soldier manages to utter one syllable. It is "*su*," the word for water, which in the regimen of Turkish grammar, is the sole irregular noun. One can suffer idiosyncracy in something so vital, so esteemed. It is Allah's greatest gift.

Since Turks who follow the proscriptions of Islam drink no alcohol, it is not surprising that they should have developed a connoisseurship of water.

And they have relinquished none of their discrimination now that theirs is a secular country where the sale and consumption of alcohol is legal. (In self-righteous Konya, where no wine is sold—on the grounds that the Koran forbids *wine*—one can buy beer and Johnny Walker scotch, neither of which the Koran specifically cites. Like Judaism and Christianity, Islam has long been given to hair-splitting, scholarly argument that strives to justify or accommodate divergent opinions and practices. All religions have their safety valves...)

When praising any of a locality's products, people are apt to exclaim that Niksar or some other town has delicious water or that a particular spring is especially sweet. I know a lady as delightful as her surname, Balpınar, which means "honey-brook."

In any new place, drinking the water is one of the rites of arrival. For better or worse, tasting the water puts the essence of a locale on the tip of one's tongue. With the goal of sampling as many springs as possible, friends of friends made a tour of Anatolia and were guided by a spirit no different from the one leading wine-lovers from one chateau to the next in Bordeaux. Credit for Turkey's good beer must be given to the refined throats of its aquaphiles.

The chronicler Evliya Çelebi, self-proclaimed teetotaler but keen taster of non-alcoholic beverages, relates that after conquering Constantinople, Sultan Mehmet asked his advisors to determine which of the local springs was the purest. By dipping equal quantities of cotton into the water at various sites, drying the skeins, and reweighing them, the sages could judge which sources held the most sediment. Since the cotton soaked in the Spring of Simon dried to the lightest weight, the Sultan declared that water most fit to drink and thereby established the preference of his descendants. In the time of the Conqueror, Evliya continues, six huge silver flagons were each day filled with the water and sealed with red wax before they were brought to the royal palace.

During Ramazan when the faithful take no food or drink, not even a sip of water, from dawn until sunset, the daytime lassitude of the towns gives way to festive evening activity. The restaurants are full, and children, wandering about with the rest of the population, play in the streets long after their customary bedtime. One night near the end of Ramazan as we visit the courtyard of the mosque of Sultan Ahmet, two little boys and a girl approach us. She is carrying a small terra cotta jug and the boys each hold a glass. "*Su*! *Su*!" calls the girl, who looks about seven years old.

Though water-sellers are still common in Istanbul, a mosque, with its communal fountain accessible to all, is a curious place to try selling water. "How much is your water?" we call to the girl.

"Only thirty lira."

"That's not cheap!" we say, and it isn't. Pointing out that there's free water here at the mosque, I tease her. "What's so special about yours, my kitten?"

"*Buz gibi.* It's like ice," she answers confidently as her unblinking minions stare at us.

"You've brought it from a special spring then?"

"No," she clicks her tongue. "It's from our own house."

"And where do you live?"

"In Çemberlitaş." Amazed that the children are nearly a mile from home at this hour, we spare her the argument that her water is doubtless the same as that running here at Sultan Ahmet. We talk and she tells us that one of the little boys is her brother, while the other is a neighbor. Her father, she says, is "a worker" and her mother "a housewife."

Enterprising children (and in a country like this, girls especially) deserve encouragement. It's more than likely we're her first customers. For one glass of water, I hand her a hundred-lira note. "Do you have change?" I ask, and of course, she doesn't. One boy holds a glass while the girl fills it to overflowing. The water is cool, but scarcely icy. There are times when one's fate is best consigned to a higher authority, so, banishing thoughts of microbes, I drain the glass before handing it back to them.

"Now," I say to the three, "you must share the hundred lira. Ask your father or your mother to break it for you. Each of the boys must have thirty lira for carrying the glasses, and you, my girl, can have forty because the water-jug is heavier. In other words, you must share the money, which is really enough for five glasses of water anywhere else in the city. You understand?" The three look appropriately grave. "*Tamam.* All right then, may your work be easy."

We bid each other good-night, and the little trio scurry off, the clapping of their plastic shoes echoing in the courtyard.

"One must not strike a snake drinking water." Even one's enemy must be spared while he partakes of that which gives life.

"May there be health!" is the proper exclamation when somone has just shaved, cut his hair, or washed.

The ablutions Muslims perform before prayer symbolize the removal of sin. They rinse their eyes, which may have looked upon the forbidden; their ears, which may have heard profane or malicious words; their mouths, which may have uttered the same; and their noses, which may have breathed the scents of unlawful substances. They wash their hands and forearms to remove any sin of reaching for what is proscribed and their feet for having strayed from the path of the Prophet. Though Allah the All-Powerful has caused the world to be riddled with enticements, in His mercy he has created water to cleanse those who fall into temptation.

Heritors of Byzantium's luxuries and Thrace's vineyards, the Turks are no strangers to temptation. Despite the austerity of Islam, there is little sanctimony among them, for along with the Mediterranean's temperate breezes, the society from the steppes has long felt the breath of Dionysius. Well-acquainted with various means of slaking thirst, the Turks are in a geographically and culturally convenient place to enjoy potables ranging from sheep's milk to a Chartreuse-like liqueur whose most noteworthy component is flaked gold.

Irreverence thrives in popular speech. The slang for *rakı*, the anise-flavored white lightning known elsehwere in the Levant as *arak*, is *imam suyu*, water (blessed by) the prayer leader. Were it not for the invariable tableside addition of real water, which clouds the liquor and cuts its fire, *rakı* would surely supply the imams with more corpses, if not more souls. The holier-than-thou are derided for the blandness of their affected piety; an underseasoned soup is said to be as tastless as the water in which an imam has performed his ablutions.

In the eastern border town of Doğubayazıt is a hotel cook of refined talents and consummate modesty. Let ironists who would dissect flowery Oriental etiquette leave this artist in peace. Having been complimented on a splendid repast, the chef shakes the hands of his well-fed clients. Lowering his eyes, he vows that to preserve the honor of having touched their hands, he will nevermore wash his!

"Health to your hands" is the standard compliment to a good cook.

As a slightly ambidextrous person with left-right orientation difficulties, I endure a few peculiar frustrations. Beginning life in North America, I learned the customary positions of the cold/right and hot/left faucets only by associating their order with the intials of my name, H. and C. Later, I managed to survive the European "C" taps that were really *caldo*, *chaud*, and *caliente*. But I knew I was in for a hard time when I found that the Turkish words for hot (*sıcak*) and cold (*soğuk*), as well as left (*sol*) and right (*sağ*) ALL begin with an "s". At first I took comfort (both cold and hot) from the tiny enamel disks colored red and blue for the temperatures they suggest. That was until I realized that their placement had been left to *kısmet* and that the hot water (regardless of the color of the dot) was usually—but not always—on the right. Then I started to come across the pairs of faucets with only red dots.... But by that time, I knew one should never assume that the landlord or hotelkeeper has obligingly turned on the hot water heater before the time one wishes to bathe....) No other features of Turkish plumbing (except for the door-locks that have trapped me in numerous bathrooms) have given me more trouble than the means by which I turn on the water. But this is no complaint. In this generally arid region, the temperature of water is not so significant as its mere existence. One is grateful for Allah's gift.

Before the prevalence of household sinks and taps, this is how a guest washed his hands before a meal: a servant (or two), circulating among the guests with a basin, ewer, and embroidered towels, would pour water over each person's hands. Fitted with a decoratively pierced plate, the basin, in the

Turkish tradition of concealing the unpleasant or the unclean, allowed the spent water to pass from sight.

Colognes and distilled waters scented with rose, lemon, or lavender continue to be offered before as well as after a meal, or even when a guest might take no more than a cup of coffee. On intercity busses, attendants dispense bottled drinking water and liberal sprinklings of cologne to their passengers, who rub it over their hands, forearms, faces and necks. And because they are associated with the religious rituals of personal hygiene, scents are peddled outside mosques by vendors with trays of chypre, jasmine, and sandalwood perfumes in tiny vials.

Anatolian busses make frequent stops, usually at establishments that are both teahouses and gas stations. Sometimes they have their own *mescit*s, small mosques, for the convenience of long-haul drivers. In those instances, one can count on the availability of water to purify the traveller and to hose down vehicles. Over the years I have evolved a means of publicly washing about seventy-five per cent of myself without removing any of the loose, full garments I wear when on the road. My genteel cat-baths have garnered a lot of laughs from truck drivers, but to the best of my knowledge, I have raised no eyebrows of disapproval and have turned no heads from Mecca.

Under the Ottomans an elaborate bureaucracy, truly one which could be described as Byzantine, evolved to ensure the urban distribution of water. Though not all remain in working order, street fountains, built to quench the thirst of man and beast, still grace many urban neighborhoods. One in (temporary?) disrepair outside an Istanbul mosque, bears the recent graffito: "If you fear Allah, don't litter here!"

And in the twentieth century, one of the cornerstones of Mustafa Kemal Atatürk's national reformation was the program whose initials appear throughout rural Turkey: Y.S.E., *yol* (roads), *su* (water), *ve elektrik* (and electricity). Crudely painted above a pipe jutting from the rocks on a road-cut or scratched into the concrete of a livestock trough, those letters or the word "*içilir*, it can be drunk" proclaim and uphold a covenant of sustenance and refreshment.

Today in Istanbul, Roman cisterns and aqueducts survive amidst Ottoman water towers, domed baths, marble fountains, and modern luxury hotels with swimming pools and sybaritic bathrooms. But even they do not epitomize the synthesis of Turkish indulgence and administrative *hubris* so well as the Ottoman regulation of water in the form of snow. Panniered pack animals carried it from the ever-white slopes of Mt. Olympus above Bursa, and boats took it across the Sea of Marmara to the capital, where the sherbet-makers at Topkapı Palace claimed the Sultan's share first. The rest of the snow harvest was recorded, taxed, sold, flavored, and finally savored by the populace. During the winter in the colder pockets of the city, it was collected where it fell, and both "imported" and local supplies were stored year-round in straw-covered pits.

That evil spirits will not follow a traveller, conscientious friends who see him off will throw a pitcherful of water in his wake to obliterate his footprints and throw the spirits off his scent.

And they say "*Su gibi gider*" may your journey, like water, flow unimpeded.

HAMAM

"The benison of hot water."
—*The Great Lover* by Rupert Brook (1887-1915)

It's high time I went to the baths. I've never been before and people always ask about them—Turkish baths, Turkish towels. In her husband's old Mercedes, I go with Tülin, a high school teacher of literature. None of my other female Turkish friends, all of whom live in modern apartments with enormous tiled bathrooms, has ever been to a *hamam*.

At first it is difficult to breathe; in that cavernous space awash with hot water the air seems to scald. Slabs of magnificent marble rippled grey and white cover the walls, the floors, and a central platform about a yard high and five by fifteen yards in area. That is the *göbek taşı*, the stomach stone. Like the floors, it is heated from below, and the water splashed everywhere steams up, caressing the naked women who recline there. Some enjoy massages, others merely lounge, smoking. Their bodies are smooth, white, and waxy—unmarked by suntan lines. Most of them have dark hair, but only on their heads. (In the antechamber, where one hears giggles from the ticklish and little gasps of endurance from the stoic, attendants depilate their clients with a taffy of lemon juice and sugar. *Il faut souffrir pour être belle.*) The bathing scene has no specific color, only tones—from wet black tresses through grey stone to white soapsuds on inner thighs. The women have arranged themselves in twos and threes, artful compositions of languorous limbs. The conversation—innuendo, rumor, assessment, endearment—condenses with the steam and drips from the domed ceiling. Sandals slap across the slippery floor, tinned copper bath bowls ring against the marble. Is it the actual heat or something else, immeasurable by Fahrenheit or Celsius, that takes my breath away? My lungs adjust as I decide Ingres' painting of *The Turkish Bath* was not far from the mark.

Having left our clothes outside in a tiny locked room and wrapped ourselves in towels (soon to be stripped away), we enter the *hamam* and take possession of a marble alcove. It is furnished with built-in seats and hot and cold taps above a *kurna*, the basin into which we dip our bowls. Pouring hot water over ourselves, we wash with chunks of yellowish old-fashioned soap. Then the *natır* leads me from the relative privacy of our alcove and lays me down on the stomach stone. A haggard mermaid with snakey hair and sagging flesh, she wears droopy black underpants into whose elastic waist she tucks scrubbing mitts, soap, and a pumice stone. Bearing down hard, she kneads and scrubs me, first with a woolen mitt, later with an orlon one. She rubs rolls of dead skin from my browned body. Finally, there's an icy dousing from her dipper with a central boss; it is exactly like the ancient libation bowls in the archeological museum here. (They say that the *natırs* lose their muscle tone from spending their lives in steam, yet Tülin, who has recently borne her first child, says she's here to regain her figure.)

Back at our own *kurna* I shampoo and lather myself a second time. Tülin asks me to splash her with cold water and then she showers me. How strange a solitary bather would seem here, like a picnic party of one. Entire families of women come, some bringing their little boys. I recall a friend saying that he used to accompany his mother and her friends to the *hamam* until one day, when he was only five, but a rather large five year-old, a gossip remarked that his mother might as well bring her husband.

Heads turbanned, bodies scrubbed to cherubic pinkness and enfolded in towels, we proceed to the drab anteroom with its vinyl furniture and order tea, sweets, manicures. Some customers have their hair set or their eyebrows tweezed. In the cubicle where we left our clothes is a narrow cot provided for napping. It is a temptation we resist today. After dressing we pay the bathing fee and tip anyone who has performed a service for us, the tea server, the *natır*, the woman with the key to our roomette. Within another hour, the baths will be swabbed and made ready for the evening, when its clientele is limited to men. It is late afternoon, early rush hour, as we ascend the staircase to the street. Glowing (and surely cleaner than I've ever been before), we return to the profane.

A year passes before I return to the same *hamam*, this time with American friends. We are washing each other when a *natır* asks me when I would like my massage. I am about to answer when a second *natır* shoves the other aside and remarks that I am her client, that she always serves me when I am there. The first shoves back and the women, forgetting my presence, argue over their rights to my blushing flesh. Both are strangers to me. Unfortunately, my three friends all know enough Turkish to comprehend what is being discussed. To terminate the imbroglio, I say that I will have neither of them, so shameful is their behavior. They sulk away, and I am left wondering for whom they mistook me.

Not long after this episode, I hear that our *hamam* is a particular favorite of local prostitutes.

In another part of Ankara, there's a placard for the direction of tourists to a building of archeological interest. Above an arrow, in red letters on white, it says "HISROTICAL BATH."

Is there any place where one could be more vulnerable to chagrin than in a *hamam*? On her first visit to Turkey, one American friend carefully selects from her Turkish phrase book words and sentences that might be useful at the baths. She copies them onto a small piece of paper and sets out accompanied only by choice phrases: "That's too hot/cold," That's not hot/cold enough," "That hurts," "Please stop that," "I must go now," and "Help!" Upon entering the scene she is immediately taken under the collective wing of several customers and bath attendants, who maneuver her through the ritual. Laughing at her swimsuit marks so pale against her tan, they scrub her with a vengeance, triumphant at the layers of "dirt" they are able to peel from her skin. Through pantomime, they indicate that the hair should be removed from her legs. As they make ready to perform the task, she knows it is for such a moment that she has brought that little list. From the plastic bag containing her shampoo and soap, she extracts the paper only to watch the ink run and the words dissolve in the steam.

Islamic tradition decrees that head-to-toe ablution is necessary after sexual intercourse. When modest Turkish women shampoo their hair at home before visiting a coiffeur, it is to keep tongues from wagging.

And what of the nineteenth-century Orientalists who painted Eastern bath tableaux populated with odalisques? (The word is from the Turkish, meaning "[girl] for the room.") Our century has accused the painters of both voyeurism and cultural misrepresentation. In their defense, I offer that few environments are more sensual than one composed of glistening wet stone and skin.

As for cultural authenticity, I came too late to find Nubian attendants in Turkish baths. And it's a pity the European painters neglected to document some especially exotic ghosts of the steam room: the felt-makers.

To produce felt, carded wool is rolled tight in reed mats and taken to the *hamam* where it is stomped upon by teams of men. Hot water, soap, and tedious pounding shrink and compact the fibers in a process known as "fulling." Following the Turkic traditions of Central Asia, the felt-makers create thick, heavy, water-repellent material for floorcoverings, saddle pads, and shepherds' capes. (On campaigns, the Ottoman armies travelled with felt tents in which they would boil cauldrons of water, thus creating portable steam baths.) But in our age of plastics, broadloom carpeting, and indoor plumbing, the odalisques seem destined to outlast the felt-makers.

"O que relumbror de novia hermoza!
...Con que lavax la vuestra cara?
Me lavo yo con agua rosada."

"Oh what sparkle, lovely bride!
...With what do you wash your face?"
I wash with rosewater."

—Traditonal Balkan wedding song in Ladino
Chants Judéo-Espagnols, Issac Levy

The *hamam* is where mothers of sons have the perfect opportunity to appraise the hips and bosoms of their future daughters-in-law, the women who will bear their grandchildren. Before the mills of Bursa turned out terry-cloth towelling, a girl's domestic accomplishments might be judged by the silk-embroidered borders of her bath linens.

In the *hamam* people have made the fabric of their lives, and dynasties have been planned amidst the soapsuds.

✷

I am swimming a slow, loopy sidestroke as I watch the wedding preparations. The water is tepid and the early evening air is freshening. A breeze ruffles the lindens, and the scent of their achingly sweet blossoms laps across the pool and surrounding terraces. The staff have been cleaning up, trying to dislodge the last sunbathers from their chaises. I have asked the lifeguard if I might stay to get a little exercise. He allows me half an hour more, and I am grateful, not so much for the exercise as for the view I have of the boys delivering garish floral displays. Rondcls of roses, gladiola, and carnations are arranged like archery targets on tripods. Each display bears a broad satin ribbon with the name of its donor sparkling in gold or silver letters (Yalcın Alkan and wife... Kent Plastics, Inc... Dr. Feyzi İğnecioğlu...) Well-wishing and advertising, together in neat bouquets.

They are setting up the tables and chairs, spreading the nappery, making a pyramid of champagne glasses, and testing the amplifiers for the band, which will be too loud even without them. Guests are already arriving, silk-draped, perfectly coiffed women who know little tricks of publicity. The photographers are in force, and women who want to be flattered by the light before dusk, before there are too many other people casting shadows, are smiling voluptuously for the cameras. There is one fellow video-taping the floral totems, panning across each one, caressing those glittering names. This is a new ritual for Istanbul, a town that is still a tribal confederation.

Knowing what else is sure to follow—the ice sculptures, the music from *The Godfather*, the waiters with flaming swords, the belly-dancer, and the bride herself in clouds of tulle—I am more captivated by the present activities. The food will be delicious, but, preferring my present vantage point, I have no longing to be included in the festivities. For the moment, this chlorinated warmth is my element, and I glide along, silent as an eel.

13

Journeys

LOCATION, LOCATION, LOCATION

In the beginning, as a traveller overwhelmed by sheer Turkishness, one cannot perceive it. Not until the foreigner resides in Turkey is he struck by the intensity of regional identifications that manifest themselves in friendly prejudice, rivalry, and anecdote. Improvements in communications and education have homogenized only certain aspects of a country whose gene pool is laced with everything from Gallic to Mongol strains. The ancient monuments of Thrace and Anatolia can distract one from the youth of this "Turkish" nation. "*Nerelisiniz*? Where are you from?" the inhabitants ask each other. As a topic of conversation, origins win out, even over food. But only just.

Neighbors deem fortunate a man whose bride is from Kayseri; not only are they are supposed to be extremely clever, but Kayseri women are famous for their yogurt-sauced *mantı* (like tiny ravioli). Everyone knows that Bolu, in the northwestern mountains, produces the best all-round chefs (who command many an embassy kitchen), but that the blue-eyed Laz (wiley or witless, depending on whose jokes one hears) from the eastern end of the Black Sea are fast acquiring a monopoly of the better Istanbul pastry shops.

With the suddenly effusive camaraderie of compatriot strangers abroad, whose shared nationality is enough to make them brothers, two young office workers recognize each other as "Istanbul men." In an Ankara restaurant, everyone else is eating steamed cracked wheat, *bulgur*, with his kebab. But the two *İstanbullu*s, each having requested rice *pilav* instead, crow with delight as they realize their common bond. Amidst much backslapping, they congratulate themselves: their choice of the more expensive, less nutritious, but more refined white rice proclaims their sophistication and sets them apart from the *bulgur*-eaters, these "peasants" chewing their way through mounds of fodder.

At the end of World War I the old city of Antep beat back French troops pressing up from Syria, thus earning the honorific title *Gazi*, "victorious fighter." Already renowned as the world's pistachio capital, Gaziantep added another feather to its turban. Over the years this seems to have rankled two nearby towns claiming to have been equally valiant in repulsing the French. Maraş, known for its curiously elastic ice cream, was a Hittite capital. Urfa, visited by both Abraham, who camped here en route to Canaan, and Caracalla, who had the misfortune to be assassinated during one sojourn, also boasts a lovely pool of sacred carp. Long on history but short on present-day publicity, Maraş and Urfa were not about to be eclipsed by just any "victorious fighter." What battles did their Chambers of Commerce wage for current road signs giving distances to "K. Maraş" and "Ş. Urfa"? But one must travel east of Adana before there is general recognition of the new names, Kahramanmaraş, "Gallant Maraş" and Şanlıurfa, "Glorious Urfa." On official road maps and on bus and airline schedules, they are never more than K. Maraş or Ş. Urfa, which read more like name-tags of petty clerks rather than a pair of irresistible destinations. Yet there sits Gaziantep printed out in all its nine-letter splendor! Is there no justice? Why, were anyone to ask for *Kahramanmaraş* ice cream, he would be laughed off the sidewalk. That pistachio baklava is still known only as "Antep baklava" is small consolation, but consolation nonetheless.

"Celery? Not the round root, you mean the long, green, American kind?" asks a friend when I wonder why I never see it sold in Ankara. "We do have it, but only in İzmir," she says. As if that should explain everything.... It doesn't. "İzmir is such a sweet city," she continues, "even the way they speak there is sweet. I love an İzmir accent." She imitates the high-vowels of that sunny, casual speech. Beach-dreaming, wine-drinking, Mediterranean Turkish. The next time I require long celery, I shall seek it, if only in spirit, in the markets of the tender city of İzmir.

Though regional identification is often expressed through food, of course, it follows other channels as well. The chairman of the board who can barely manage a dog-paddle in the Hilton pool is teased for being an "Anatolian boy." That he settled permanently on the shores of Istanbul when he was a youngster is remembered less well than that he was born in Konya, where the nearest body of water is a salt lake so shallow that in summer it can be crossed on foot.

Where but Istanbul could one die because the prow of a Bosphorus ferryboat smashed through the wall of one's dining room? It is the consummately chic demise because everyone knows what waterfront property costs these days.

Is there a border town anywhere that enjoys a good reputation? Not Niagara Falls or Tijuana or Ceuta. Well, maybe Geneva. But certainly not Kars glaring across at what was the Soviet Union from the northeastern corner of Turkey. Brooding, even under the clear skies of the high plateau, the dark basalt stones of Kars's buildings have been caught in crossfire too often. Even the Chekovian gingerbread, left from the last of the Russian occupations, fails to jollify this garrison settlement.

If there's a border, I want to set foot on the other side. Or come as close as I can. So as to stand amidst the ruins of the medieval Armenian city of Ani along the gorge of the Arpa River that cuts between Turkey and formerly-Soviet Armenia, I've endured a morning in Kars—twice.

Like nomads in search of pasture for their flocks, my friends and I have passed our Turkish times in motion. Nineteenth-century travelogues, modern maps and archeological reports, other friends' accounts, and our own curiosity lure us from our desks, push and pull us across Turkey. Our restlessness is invariably rewarded, but in my case, at least, it can never be satisfied. I confess that the scent of the unknown encounter—diesel fuel—excites me. Whether at a modern airport or a scruffy bus terminal, the smell quickens my reflexes and tempts me to get on the conveyance headed for Damascus even though I have a ticket back to Istanbul. I am incorrigible.

Places where things once happened, but where no five-star hostelries are under construction, are the places that draw me most. Alone and with companions, I have gone into Thrace and southeastern Anatolia, to towns forgotten, mishandled, or undiscovered by the Ministry of Tourism. Mere ticket-counter destinations to some, they've been Meccas to me.

EDİRNE

"Little soul, wandering, gentle guest and companion of the body, into what places will you now go..."

—*Ad Animam Suam*, Hadrian (A.D. 76-138)

Now it's the E5, the Londra Asfaltı, but it was once the Via Egnatia and led to Rome. Alongside the road, the Emperor Hadrian built himself a city, which the Greeks called Adrianopolis. Less mellifluously, the Turks have rendered the name "Edirne." It's a drowsy border town where, as Larry Butler says, "It's still 1913 and everyone is waiting for news from the front." Indeed, the Balkan Question seems unanswered in Edirne with its Hellenic merchants' houses (pediments and architraves painted salmon, blue, and yellow), overhanging Slavic stories, and magnificent Ottoman mosque complexes. One can walk to Greece and take a taxi to the Bulgarian border, but few in the late twentieth century would argue that the town, with its scarved women and vaulted caravanserais, is anything but Turkish.

And a country town where one counts as many horse carts as Mercedes trucks. It's small and so welcomes the pedestrian. A half-dozen of us walk, heading northwest of the road that goes to Bulgaria, leaving the paved streets behind us as we reach the edge of town and the meadows along the River Tunca. We're headed for the mosque complex, the *külliye*, of Beyazit the Second that lies across the river. A young soldier with a shaved head is slouched against the railing of the bridge we need to cross. As we approach, he adjusts the shoulderstrap of his rifle and comes to attention before uttering the favorite word of all people who possess a modicum of authority: "*Yasak*," he says. Forbidden.

"*Selam aleykum*," we greet him.

The Turkish dictum of civility to strangers transcends any army regulations. "*Aleykum selam*," he replies sullenly.

Not forgetting that it is Ramazan and that the soldier has probably fasted since dawn, we say, "May your hours pass swiftly and easily." Bewildered, for nothing in his experience has prepared him for conversation with foreigners, he is conditioned by convention and reflex to thank us. And he does so because it requires no effort.

He points to our cameras. "*Yasak*."

"But we can cross the bridge to the *külliye*?" We emphasize the positive.

"No photographs."

"No photographs of what?"

"The bridge." It seems unbelievable that at this juncture the Turkish military would consider crucial a bridge over water a wader could ford. Nevertheless, Mehmet here has his orders.

"But we can photograph the *külliye*?" He nods. We concoct floridly polite phrases of gratitude and are about to proceed when the soldier stiffens and takes hold of his rifle. We follow his gaze, and then we see her a bit down stream, our absent-minded museum curator focussing a lens on two ducks gliding under the bridge. We shout to her, but she seems not to hear. The soldier raises his weapon to his shoulder. We shout again and our friend is startled by our expressions...and the gun.

Together, we all take leave before the soldier has second thoughts. We cross over the Tunca, a river with a current barely perceptible as it flows through this suspect terrain.

Exurbis development was common practice among Ottoman city planners; and in the 1480's Beyazit built his mosque, soup kitchens, medical school, hospital, and insane asylum across the river, to encourage the expansion of Edirne. But today Beyazit's white marble *külliye* is still beyond the town and lies all but abandoned in a pasture of red poppies and wheat gone wild. A handful of villagers still visit the mosque. We find it locked until prayer time, so wander through the uncut grass to the hospital. The *külliye*, supported by rents and revenues from its land-holdings, provided medical attention, special foods, and fragrant flowers for the infirm and insane. This afternoon nesting pigeons burble beneath the asylum's beautiful dome, where musicians played to soothe the mad and melancholy. We pause, listening for echoes. Leaving the asylum we come upon a leggy, weed-choked chrysanthemum plant beside a wall. I pinch it back that it might bloom more profusely and comfort ailing spirits.

> "Think, in this batter'd Caravanserai
> Whose Portals are alternate Night and Day,
> How Sultan after Sultan with his Pomp
> Abode his destin'd Hour and went his way."

—*The Rubaiyat of Omar Khayyam*
Edward Fitzgerald, 1879

We stroll back to town, negotiating the gypsy quarter en route. Leaning on door jambs, bareheaded women smoke and call out to us to take coffee with them. Their earrings swing as they laugh. Their Turkish (mixed with Romany?) is hard to understand, and, unfairly, we imagine them making ribald jests at our expense. Dishevelled children shriek at hopscotch or soccer; a dog and her litter nap under the shade of unpruned roses. Loading grain sacks onto a flat-bed truck, a buxom, braless girl in a T-shirt and *şalvar* works with her brothers. What would they say in straight-laced Konya, where they even malign the dervishes as libertines? Surely nothing good about the gypsies...except, maybe, for Deli Selim (Crazy Selim) and his band with its raucous clarinets.

But is Deli Selim, one of Edirne's favorite sons, really a gypsy? What good belly-dance musician isn't? Could it be that only a gypsy is shameless enough to abandon himself to music ordinary people merely love at arm's length?

"...they are called Zingarri; they are either found wandering amongst deserts or mountains, or settled in towns, supporting themselves by horse-dealing or

jugglery, by music and song. In no part of the East are they more numerous than in Turkey...where the females frequently enter the harems of the great, pretending to cure children of 'the evil eye,' and to interpret the dreams of the women. They are not unfrequently [*sic*] seen in the coffee-houses, exhibiting their figures in lascivious dances to the tune of various instruments; yet these females are by no means unchaste, however their manners and appearance may denote the contrary, and either Turk or Christian who, stimulated by their songs and voluptuous movements, should address them with proposals of a dishonourable nature, would, in all probability, meet with a decided repulse."

—*The Zincali* by George Borrow, 1843

THE SOUTHEAST

"One should take one's ruins carefully, in small doses between meals."

—Freya Stark, *Letters from Syria*, 1928

Fleeing the November rains of Istanbul, our plane skirts the aquamarine lakes near Eğridir and makes short work of the Plateau. Palm trees and the silver meanders of the Seyhan and Ceyhan deltas greet us as we descend to Adana. This is my favorite sort of trip, an almost-unmapped adventure with a few friends. For the next week, we'll drive around southeastern Anatolia in the Fiat sedan we've rented at the airport.

Humid summers are to blame for the ever-peeling paint on Adana's concrete apartment buildings. Modern industrial sprawl and roads choked by commercial truck traffic contribute to the city's chronic shabbiness. Statistics indicate Adana is Turkey's second or third richest city, but I've never found anything that made me want to linger here. Before we escape the tangled traffic, a pushcart laden with good-looking dates has pulled alongside us. "How much a kilo?" I ask.

"Seven hundred lira, *Abla*" comes the vendor boy's reply as we inch through the congestion and leave him behind. "All right, five hundred," he shouts. I should succumb, but I don't. And we do not see their quality again, at any price.

Just outside the city, we drive through a herd of black goats (their long horns painted blue for good luck) and see women plucking the cotton bolls left behind by the mechanical pickers in use everywhere now.

We leave the main road to visit the mosaic museum in the hamlet of Misus. The sign, the usual yellow historical arrow, is well-rusted, as if it's been up for years, but the museum, except for a tin roof, is yet to be erected. A solitary watchman shows us where the mosaics lie, deliberately covered by layers of straw and soil, so no one will suspect their existence and try to pry them up for private gain.

A pine-shaded road now leads into Ceyhan, no longer the sleepy delta town I remember from a dozen years ago. Today we drive through a city of more than 100,000 and pause outside a shop whose sign says "Sesame, Bought and Sold." We ogle what must be half a ton of toasted seeds poured into the corner of the small, street-front shop. The going retail price in downtown Ceyhan? Seven hundred the kilo, less than a dollar a pound. Fortunately food, in all its forms, is among the many interests we four travellers share.

Doubling back on the road, we stop at Yılankalesi, Snake Castle, one of those ruined fortifications accentuating the dragonback ridges that rise from the Cilician Plain. The oldest foundations are Roman, if not earlier. Is that Byzantine brick beneath chronological courses of Armenian, Crusader, Selcuk, and Ottoman masonry? Sometimes the indefinition of such places enhances the pleasure they give, absolves one of the necessity to know the facts of the great Mideastern mélange. This afternoon it is enough to understand the concept of "Castle." Unlike our companion David, I do not even feel compelled to climb it. I have on the wrong sandals and stop midway. There are mauve autumn crocus, large and delicate, growing in clusters of three and four. A few heart-shaped cyclamen leaves, what I take for tulip leaves, and some bright blue members of the borage family, too. From the base of a watchtower, I've a placid view of patched fields. The mid-afternoon *ezan* drifts up from the village below. No, I don't need to climb the parapets.

The highway to Gaziantep goes through surprisingly green and hilly areas, so densely wooded they remind me of the Black Sea regions. We are saddled with a lot of truck traffic and spend hours passing diesel belchers on steep inclines. Nonetheless, we enter Gaziantep well before dusk and are routed into town via a new road that gives us a look at scores of as-yet-unoccupied apartment buildings. (Quite luxurious, mostly five and six stories, generous balconies; I guess that there are probably ten to fifteen apartments per building.) Over this new road, stands a ceremonial arch bearing the words, "The legless and armless are our living martyrs." A weird welcome to what proves to be a cheerful, generous city.

To find the hotel where we have reservations, we ask directions of a young motorcyclist alongside us at a stop-light. He does the gracious, *Turkish* thing, which is to ride ahead and lead us there through the motorbikes and trucks that will defy our ear-plugs tonight. I swear this is the noisiest city in Turkey.

After settling in, we decide to try the hotel dining room. Invited into the kitchen beforehand, we select delicious *meze*, which include green olive and hot pimento salad and *muhammara*—a spread of ground walnuts, bread, olive oil, and fresh, sweet red peppers. There are also cooked red peppers, cold, stuffed with rice. Only the wine is pricey, about four times what it would be in a shop. As we leave for an after-dinner stroll, we pass the bar, really no more than a wall display of fancy bottles. We ask if what seems to be a flask of Poire William, complete with the pear, is genuine. The bartender laughs, explaining that once it was, but now that the original *eau de vie* is gone, the manager has refilled the container with local gin!

Immediately outside the hotel is a row of shops packed with Antep's *fıstık* (pistachio) specialities, famous and obscure—pistachio paste, various kinds of *baklava*, *kadayıf*, *burma*....

We poke our heads inside one shop, and young employees push samples of all their confections upon us. There is a hardened nougat with toasted chickpeas, crispy semi-sweet sheets of unroasted sesame, and a vapid white walnut taffy (of which David, in his usual enthusiasm, buys half a kilo!). One thing seems too rich to even contemplate: pistachio paste layered with sesame *helva*.

Around the corner is what we dub "The Doctors' Street" for its scores of office placards projecting over the sidewalks. Among the gynecologists and X-ray technicians, we are surprised to note no undue number of dentists or specialists in diabetes, called "sugar sickness" in Turkish.

Having worked up a slight appetite for a sit-down dessert, we make our first foray into the gleaming shop of the Güllüoğlü family, where we order portions of *fıstık* baklava and tea. The boys serving are clearly descended from the photo gallery hanging above the counter—three generations of Mongol, semi-Mongol, and twentieth-century urban Turk. It is an amazing demonstration of Anatolia as a melting pot. After tasting their sweets, one imagines that all had to have been first-rate pastry chefs!

Gaziantep's vitality stems from real commerce —smuggling, smithing, spices, sweetmeats—not the contrived activities of tourism. The lanes of the vast market area are not organized along the usual groupings of tradesmen: spice merchants are neighbors of jewelers and shoemakers.

Years ago Antep was the black market par excellence—for Soviet watches, Ford hubcaps, and kitchen appliances. (Borders breed smugglers and Syria lies less than an hour away.) But with the 1980's liberalization of government economic controls, legal imports have caused a smuggling slump. As for the other traditional industries—condiments and confections are holding their own. The ringing of smithies fills the air.

Except for a small cloth bazaar and the *hal* of butchers and spice sellers, where men (arms vermilion to the elbow) mix red pepper paste with their hands, the pistachio and honey *han* is one of Antep's few covered markets.

Nut brokers, impassive behind dark glasses, wait for deals to materalize. Their one-room shops, nestled in stone walls enclosing a tree-shaded courtyard, must have looked much the same in the days of camel caravans. A few dim niches house stores of honey and *pekmez*. A thick syrup made from boiled-down grape or pomegranate juice, *pekmez* is sold in reused *rakı* bottles. Different wildflower honeys, still in the comb, sit in open tins.

One honey merchant insists I guess his age. To be polite, I venture "45" though he looks ten years older. Smiling broadly, he credits his youthful "54 years!" to a thick, greenish honey in which bits of leaf matter are suspended. "Three spoonfuls of this thyme honey, and I can drink half a bottle of *rakı* every night!" He dips his finger into an open crock while offering me a tasting spoon. "Good for coughs," he says.

There is not an insect in sight, and one speculates on the nature of the toxic sprays that must maintain this absence of ants, flies, and fleas, especially since huge bales of unwashed sheep's wool rest beneath the branches of stout mulberry and *çınar* trees in the courtyard. At first I cannot fathom why wool would be sold beside dry nuts and fruits. Then someone explains that to barter for comestibles, shepherds have brought wool shorn from their flocks. It would be fascinating to know how much a kilo of uncarded wool is worth in terms of any of the goods for sale here—dried apricots, raisins, prunes, beans, walnuts....

We wander, following our noses to a stall selling strong perfumes. I ask to sample some "rose" and am liberally daubed with a ghastly synthetic. (Maybe this is what has eradicated the city's insect life.) Heidi wants a whiff of the shopkeeper's best-seller, and he proudly sprays something labelled "Brute," which "comes from Istanbul." In Gaziantep, that is as good as coming from Paris.

On a typical Anatolian market street of wooden toy-makers, spoon-sellers, and saddlers, a wagon filled with polished eggplants, tomatoes, and red onions is picturesquely parked against a backdrop of pale poplar-wood wares. But this morning I have left behind my camera; I like less and less to wear the albatross. We also see makers of what I call "dervish boots," the little high-rise black leather slippers that someone besides the Mevlevi dervishes must wear (but who?). Are these Turkish "at home" wear? Then there are the beautiful, sturdy red shoes, some with turned up toes, all with the permanent scent of the tannery. They hang in bunches, and like the famous Antep red peppers they mimic, cry for the camera lens.

On the other side of the color wheel are the cartloads of fresh green olives. We keep running into the same vendor; it's not that I remember him so much as his olives, which seem larger and greener than any others we pass. On the fourth encounter, I ask him how the locals cure green olives. He says that all they do is crack the flesh before soaking them in fresh water. To keep the olives completely submerged, fig leaves are laid atop the water's surface. After fifteen days, he says, the olives are ready to eat. A trio of onlookers agree that this is the local custom. I find it hard to believe, unless the water here is terribly alkaline....

Above all else, this is a gastronomic bazaar. Restaurant fronts are still-lifes that might have been assembled by the unlikely team of Bosch and Chardin. One has pyramids of tomatoes and lemons, crossed rapiers of raw ground meat molded and decoratively crimped on the skewers, and little boiled lambs' heads, baring their tiny teeth above collars of parsley.

We go through the cheese and butter streets. Interspersed are plastic dishpan sellers and herbalists with bunches of dried blue gentian (for diabetes, they inform us). Across the way is a hunter's shop with badly taxidermied birds and a hyena skin hanging on a peg. We find a fellow selling several varieties of dry snacks, and discover that Antep, not suprisingly, has roasted chickpeas dusted with hot red pepper. Our marathon of tasting begins here when the proprietor presses sugared *leblebi* upon us. Another similar stall has rosy, unhusked pistachios strung and hung beside its door. There we sample the nuts before we buy a quarter kilo as strolling fuel. We also try the crunchy turquoise seeds of *Pistacia terebinthus*, which the Turks call *menengiç*. Their flavor lies somewhere between pistachios (to which they are related) and juniper berries, which they resemble.

We pause before the window of a baklava bakery to watch boys sorting pistachios on a marble-topped counter, and the door is thrown open to welcome us into the butter-scented warmth. By chance, this is the bakery for the Güllüoğlü shop we patronized the previous evening. Samples, really full-size servings, are handed to each of us as we inspect thc wood-fired ovens that bake 100-200 kilos of baklava each day. Going through tubs of flavorful butter brought from nearby Urfa, these bakers fill special orders and restock the various Güllüoğlü shops in Gaziantep.

There's a chill drizzle to keep us hungry. At a simple, bustling restaurant I order *lahmacun*, a thin paste of lamb, onion, herbs and hot pepper spread on dough and baked like a pizza. David, Alice, and Heidi order kebabs and stews, pickles and salads. Suddenly there is an embarrassingly large number of plates on our table.

After lunch, we take in the regional museum, a better-than-usual collection of archeological finds and ethnographia. In one case I spot a pair of silk-embroidered panels executed in a technique I'd previously assumed to be Palestinian. If only I could unfold the textiles, pinned to the fabric-covered back of the case.... The door to the case is unlocked, openable. I summon the guard. "My dear uncle," I begin, explaining I would like to see the textiles more closely. He is fearful, but allows me to open the case and finger the fabric. However, he won't let me unpin it to determine whether it is a tunic or trousers panel. How frustrating! But I understand his position. I ask if I might see the director, to ask his permission.

The guard gladly sees me up to the director's office. A pleasant-looking man with a double chin and prematurely grey hair, the director orders tea for me. I sense that this no more than obligatory courtesy.

Taking care to avoid the red-flag word *araştırma*, or "research," I put forward my request. Nonetheless, the director clicks his tongue and says I must have a research permit from the Ministry of Culture in Ankara. To touch a piece of fabric seventy years old? How do such uncreative thinkers rise to become bureaucrats in provinces where they have the final say? To protect the accommodating guard, I say nothing of the fact that the case is already unlocked.

I ask the director for his card and he gives me one stained with old glue. It lists his profession not as director, but as "archeologist." I ask him of his specialty. He answers, "Classical, Greek and Roman."

" Alas," I commiserate with him, "and here you are in southeastern Anatolia, so far from Ephesus and Pergamum!" I expcct a rueful laugh, at least, or perhaps a polite inquiry into my own background.

But there are no bites from this fish out of water. Clearly, my unannounced appearance has disturbed his *keyif*. A telephone intercom on his desk sends out waves of noise: saws, sledgehammers pounding, men shouting. (We had noticed work being done on a new wing of the museum). So this is how the director keeps on top of things.

I notice a detailed city map on his wall and stand up to examine it. I ask which are the most interesting parts of the old city. The director rises and, with difficulty, finds the museum on the map before he indicates the historic neighborhoods. (By and large, I judge Turkish map-reading skills to be negligible.) It is time for me to depart, and in my most flowery Turkish, I thank him for his help. As I leave, he mentions that were I able to get a permit, I might be able to view the much richer holdings in storage, "things no one ever sees," he says. Or will ever see, at this rate.

Having debated whether to walk the old streets now, in the rain, or to hope for a sunny morning, we seize the daylight, murky and fading fast. The streets, with their finely cut stone houses, remind me of lanes in Arab medinas. Little ogee windows pierce the walls, and arches with colored voussoirs span the cobbled alleys, muddy, but free of refuse. We reach the lowest part of the castle fortifications and find ourselves in an open square where we can admire the minarets lit against the night

The minarets in Antep (and Urfa, too) are decorated with plates and bowls set into the well-fitted stone. With my binoculars, I pick out some Canton, Imari, and Blue Willow. I wonder if there were earlier adornments of Persian and Turkish wares, long since stolen or dislodged in earthquakes. None of the guide books makes any mention of this curious, local ornamentation.

Unshaded bulbs of clear glass and kerosene lanterns keep the bazaar going after dark. We are offered a slice of persimmon as a merchant explains how to make stuffed cabbage and pickled cabbage, but doesn't really answer the question: what is done with the tons and tons of cabbage we see mounded in Antep's market. Grudgingly, he admits that "women probably know other uses" for the vegetable.

We wriggle through the evening rush hour traffic until we find ourselves in a metalworking han. Arches around the courtyard frame medieval scenes of coppersmiths, their cauldrons and trays glinting in wavering torch-light. Our century seems far-removed.

The next morning, we are prevented from climbing around the Antep citadel, which is enjoying extensive restoration. I've no idea how faithful a restoration it will be—one must make hard choices in these undertakings: which layers of civilization are to be sacrificed, which to be saved. Under a cloudless sky, an ad hoc poultry market has sprung up beside the walls of the castle. In a nearby cookshop, David and Alice sit down to chicken soup. But I, even after years in Turkey, have not developed a taste for breakfast soup.

Instead, Heidi and I find a shop where the Antep breakfast specialty, *katmer*, is being rolled out on a marble slab. Taking stools in the tiny bakery, we watch the chef roll the elastic dough to transparency before he spreads it with moistened, slightly sweetened semolina. The dough is folded, brushed with butter, and baked in an oven that is no more than a sheet-steel box fired by gas jets. As soon as it is baked, the pastry is liberally sprinkled with—what else?—ground pistachios. A sublime way to start the day.

Heidi and I walk up above the bazaar through more old streets. A courtyard door is ajar to a charming scene of fruit trees, potted flowers, and drying laundry. We peer inside and are welcomed with kisses from a plump, jolly woman our own age. She begs us to have tea with her but we bow out, now, and as we shall so many times during this trip, in the pursuit of some other goal to be achieved within the next few minutes, hours, or days.

This morning we are headed for a twin-minaretted mosque I've spied from below. We reach it without difficulty, but find it locked until prayer-time. No matter, the walk's the thing. In the adjaceant park old men sit in the sun. Each bench-warmer greets us with *selam aleykum* and an exhortation to enjoy the view over the plains of pistachio trees and vineyards. Before we make our way down the hill, past houses with strangely carved stone pillars (with capitals like pairs of cornucopias), we stop to photograph white-collared school-children at a grocery store. Some are buying bread to take home to their mothers, others are choosing candies. The grocer asks that I send him a photo and writes his address for me. An older man (I can't tell whether he's a customer or co-owner) makes me a present of the largest apple I have ever seen.

No more than half an hour out of Gaziantep, white blocks tumbling over a low *höyük* attract our attention. We drive half a mile on a muddy, wagon-rutted road which winds into the village named Şekili. Through an open door, I catch a glimpse of hands rolling out *yufka*. We stop, bounding out of the car as women and children spill out the door. Among them stands a stout blond wearing heavy eye-liner. I greet her and she shakes my hand with some hesitation. Then an older woman gives me a kiss on each cheek, grasps my hand in her leathery palm, and pulls me into the courtyard.

Two smiling women are making the flat bread, one rolling out the dough, the other toasting it quickly on a *saç*, a convex iron griddle. They are in a white-washed corner, closed off with translucent plastic sheeting that keeps out drafts and keeps in the smoke of the wood fire. The even light, glowing coals, white smoke, stucco, and speckled sheets of whole wheat bread make a beautiful chiaroscuro, if potentially tubercular, scene. I hold my breath, photograph, and then greedily chew on the warm bread so enthusiastically offered.

The little legion of people has crowded inside the courtyard with us. My friends are chatting with the blond woman, married to the man in the black *şalvar.* She's a German, from Spandau outside Berlin, and has lived in this village only six months, after ten years of married life in her homeland. (The three scampering blonds with Turkish names are her children). She seems dazed by our arrival and my friends' ability to speak her native tongue. She volunteers haphazard information about herself: "I weighed two tons when I came, but it's so hot here in summer that I can't even think about food" and "I am not accustomed to this bread."

Up on the flat roof are a score of tame pigeons; the white ones have flight feathers dyed bright cerise. In the sharp sunlight, I realize that each has something glittering at the neck. I climb the narrow stairs built into the courtyard wall (and think, as all the children below peek up my skirt, that this is one of the rare times I would have been more comfortable in trousers).

Upon closer inspection of the birds, I find myself once more thrilled by a never-before and perhaps never-again sight in this land: each of the pigeons is wearing jewelry! Their necks have been pierced to carry what looks like an earring, a crescent with pendant gold-colored spangles and red glass beads. Then I notice that the flock all wear beads on their "ankles" as well! The beads are large-holed and must have been slipped over the feet of the birds when they were younger. We ask if the pigeons' decorations are against the Evil Eye or for mere adornment. We don't get a clear answer. The solution of such mysteries often demands a longer visit than we can make.

Back on the Urfa road, we pass Nizip, a Cubist white city that might have been snipped from North Africa. But we save it for the future as we press on, following the yellow historical signs to Karkamış (Carchemish), the Hittite capital whose citadel ruins lie on what is now the Syrian border. There are yellow signs, too, for Jerablus. Odd, since it is across the border, definitely within Syria. Why are the Turks giving their none-too-dear neighbors free publicity, I wonder.

The land is almost perfectly flat as we drive south. The aspect of the usual treeless, mud-walled village makes us thankful we weren't born peasants here. Suddenly, right along the road is a completely different village, still mud, but mud beautifully smoothed to form crenellated walls and fanciful roof ornaments. We beg David to slow down, and as he does, two old tatooed Kurdish women in purple and saffron headscarves appear. Our runnning joke about "photo opportunity!" is repeated for the nth time, and we stop.

I hurry out before the women can vanish (I've known some Kurdish women to be particularly skittish). "*Selam aleykum*!" we call, knowing that they'll understand the Arabic greeting even if they don't know Turkish. They extend their hands and would be pleased to have us shake them. Instead, just to make absolutely certain they know we come with good intentions, I kiss each hand and press it to my forehead, the gesture of respect and humility reserved for one's seniors. Each woman then kisses me on both cheeks (and I get a close-up of their tatoos, indigo chevrons and dots at the temples and chin). We've been accepted. (It is only later that I ask myself if I'm a shameless exhibitionist. The hand-kissing probably wasn't necessary, though it certainly gave pleasure to everyone involved.)

Heidi and I split off from Alice and David, who are quickly captured and taken into the most beautiful of the mud houses. This is how we divide and conquer, observing different things and sharing our discoveries later. And this is what we find here in the village of Çoksuruk (old name) or Yolağızı (new name meaning "mouth of the road"): The people speak Kurdish, Turkish, and Arabic, but consider themselves to be Turks. The women's dress of full petticoats and double headscarves (one tied across the forehead as a band) is typically "K." We euphemize, so we can speak openly of various groups and avoid offending anyone (the Turks are "T," the Arabs and Armenians "A").

Large round sieves strung with leather or gut are used to sift the earth that will be mixed with water to provide the smooth facing of the buildings and walls. Mud bricks are drying in wooden molds set out in the sun. Mud cones are built up around saplings to protect them from wind, moisture loss, and gluttonous goats.

Miniscule gardens are walled in, too; a plot scarcely larger than a prayer rug boasts a row of peas, a rose bush, and green onion shoots. Entry is gained through a wooden gate that is so small and low it seems built for an animal, not a gardener.

The buildings here are honey-colored and some have wooden window and door frames painted yellow or blue as brilliant as the sky is for me, here, today....

Stepping out of our shoes, we join Alice and David inside the home of Ayna Hanım, who explains that she decorated the house herself, when she was a young bride. It is bright and cheerful with a blue, yellow, red, and green plate rack she painted with birds and flowers. The rack holds a collection of stencilled metal soup bowls.

On divans covered with cross-stitched cottons, about fifteen villagers—men, women and children—have gathered around Alice and David to chat and listen. Alice asks about the kilim rug on the floor; Ayna says she wove it eight years ago to serve as her late husband's shroud when he was carried to the mosque. We drink tea, take photographs, write down names and addresses.

Leaving, I take a while to put on my long-laced walking shoes. As I sit awkwardly in the doorway, the women touch my hair and comment on its color.

We escape having to stay for a meal ("We'll cook a lamb for you!") with the white lies that we have just eaten, that we are full of our picnic food, and that if only we had known we would find so hospitable a village, we would have waited. "Come back, then," they chorus. *İnşallah*, we shall, and that is an earnest wish. As we drive away, a little girl hands a nosegay of pungent marigolds through our window.

The fly-blown town of Karkamış (we see no flies, but it is the sort of place that one would definitely describe that way) does not intrigue us as we shop its only commercial stretch for tea glasses, paper napkins, fresh *pide*, white cheese, tomatoes, and wine. There is a surprisingly extensive selection of undusty bottles in one grocery. Do Syrians steal across the border for an occasional rosé or are the Turkish Army officers the grocer's main customers?

We should stock up here, for reliable labels will be harder to find in the coming days. But we buy only two bottles; in the provinces, one never knows whether any wine is good. Most of the provincial grocers do not drink wine themselves and have never learned how to care for the bottles they sell. How often one finds bottles stored beside kerosene heaters....

We continue to follow yellow signs that lead us along a weak tributary of the Euphrates and then come up against the all-too-familiar, diagonally striped red and white *Yasak Bölge* fencing that marks a forbidden zone, a military installation. Three enlisted men saunter over to the car and one of them, friendly in a cocky way as he blows cigarette smoke through our window, says that when the commandant comes back we might ask him for a permit to visit the Hittite ruins which lie at the heart of the military compound. Heidi, Alice, David, and I all agree that there is no way we are going to kill the rest of our lovely afternoon waiting for any sort of permit. After two winning villages, we are quite prepared to cut our losses and depart Karkamış in search of a picnic spot. It's nearly three and we're ravenous.

Just before we regain the main road to Urfa, we settle ourselves in an olive grove and spread out lunch. The white wine proves exceptional, a worthy toast to the roads we've taken and to the way that lies ahead.

IN MESOPOTAMIA

On Turkish intercity busses, the seats behind the driver are invariably given to single female travellers. So installed, I view an excess of oncoming traffic, but benefit from more fresh air, as the driver's window is usually open—a good thing, since during the journey he and many passengers will smoke. (But things are changing, even in tobacco-growing Turkey, where there's a new concern for the perils of cigarettes.)

A young boy acting as steward offers bottles of cold spring water and inaugurates the journey by sprinkling lemon cologne into the cupped hands of passengers. It's a custom more heart-felt and refreshing than the airlines' hand-out of foil-wrapped Wash'n Dries.

It is two years since my last visit to the southeast. I am sleepy after lively, but late-night chatting with a Gaziantep journalist impassioned by the issues of heroin smuggling, Armenian-Turkish détente, and CIA infiltration of Protestant church missions in Turkey. Beside me sits a young nurse named Aliye, on leave from the State hospital in Antakya, near the Mediterranean coast. She is thin and pale with a blemished complexion. I decline the cheese bun she offers me; she folds it up in newspaper and leans her head on the cushioned railing in front of our seats.

"I was the duty nurse last night," she explains, "and the bus from Antakya left at eight this morning." Three hours later, when I board the bus, we become *yoldaş*, literally "road sisters," in the Gaziantep bus station. Tacitly, Aliye and I leave each other to private repose, and she closes her eyes. Afraid that I might miss something, I rarely doze when journeying here.

It is mid-September in what used to be called Kurdistan, and I'm off to try to fill a gap in my Turkish experience, namely the city of Diyarbakır about an hour and a half north of the Syrian border. Because seven months from now I'll be leading a small tour through the eastern provinces, I have special incentive to explore that city. Not only must I consider where twenty people will lodge and dine, but I must also have an idea of what we should plan to see. I've been there but once, in 1985, and then just to change planes. While in the terminal, I saw a military honor guard carrying the coffin of a Turkish soldier said to have died in an Iraqi border skirmish involving Kurdish guerrillas. Only from the air have I viewed Diyarbakır: low, atop a small butte rimmed with fortifications of dark grey basalt, whose medieval defense towers and crenellations seemed very much intact. The town overlooks cultivated patches along the Tigris, an aqua ribbon snaking slowly south to Baghdad and beyond. Ever since that glimpse, I've wanted to return.

In Gaziantep, I've been told that Diyarbakır has reported a hundred cases of malaria this year, though just a few years ago it was widely believed that the disease had been eradicated in Turkey. As a hasty prophylaxis, I've swallowed a pill of chloroquine diphosphate and will assay the situation when I arrive. My skin feels papery, and it is hard to imagine mosquitos thriving in the aridity of Anatolia in late summer. But the Tigris is not the only river to rise in Turkey; and mosquitos breed in irrigation ditches.

Fifteen miles east of Gaziantep our bus passes the village of Şekili. Remembering the spangled pigeons, I wonder if the German woman has acquired a taste for her in-laws' flat bread. I cannot return there today. Another time, in a private car, yes. Faster, cheaper, and safer than private cars, busses have their constraints and reveal fewer secrets.

Reaching Mesopotamia half an hour later, we cross the Euphrates at Birecik, its sand-colored fortress built into the left bank above the jaded waters and tufts of willow on summer shoals. Nearby, in July of 1911, a foot-sore T. E. Lawrence, yet to become "El Orans" of Arabia, washed out his spare shirt.[†]

Just two hours out of Gaziantep, we pull into the bus station of Urfa for what is euphemistically called a tea break. The toilets are Asian-style, reasonably clean, with lots of running water. Aliye and I take turns holding each other's purses. When

[†]These were Lawrence's days as an amateur archeologist and bazaar-prowler described in *Oriental Assembly*, published posthumously by E.P. Dutton, 1940. According to the author's brother, T.E. had once referred to writing up the journal of this trip as something entitled *Seal-Hunting in Mesopotamia*, a piece never found in print or manuscript form.

we are finished we wash our hands, and I notice how thoroughly she lathers hers and then scoops water over the tap before she finally touches it to turn it off. Nurse's training, no doubt. The lavatory attendant in a booth outside waits to collect the equivalent of six cents from each departing customer. Aliye steps ahead of me and insists on paying my tariff. Always insistent, Turkish hospitality takes some droll turns.

In Urfa, Lawrence suffered an abcessed wisdom tooth and wrote that he "quieted it" with rose sherbet. Today, in the shade of the station, sits a vendor with a block of ice and a bottle of viscous pink syrup. Using a knife, he shaves off half a glassful of ice, adds some syrup and water, and hands me the concoction. Rose it is, and sweet enough to *give* one a toothache, but I cannot resist a silent toast to Lawrence and expatriate eccentricity. Aliye declines my invitation to sip sherbet, but accepts a peeled, salted cucumber proffered by another vendor. (Finely ribbed, pale green, and curved like a sickle, it appears in Burpee's Seed Catalogue as "Armenian," and is touted for its thin skin and lack of bitterness.)

A tiny bazaar of glassware, cheap clothing, costume jewelry, and other accessories has been set up inside the station. We wander around and Aliye haggles for a leather coin purse. In the midst of the scene is a wheeled cart with trays of Urfa's specialty—*çiğ köfte*, oval meatballs of raw lamb highly seasoned with black pepper, green onions, garlic, cinnamon, mint, and Urfa's distinctive roasted paprika. Aliye says she adores them and asks if I do, too. I answer that although I've enjoyed them made to order in restaurants, I feel that one has to draw the line somewhere and that a hot bus station selling raw meat is where I draw mine. Since she's a nurse, I'm surprised when she gives me a puzzled look.

We reboard the bus along with a new contingent of long-nosed Kurdish families and a quartet of Europeans. Two boys, who speak English with Teutonic accents, are clean-cut in chinos and T-shirts. The girls are British, with beautiful faces and dirty Indian-print clothing; the bus station crowd has been staring at the hirsute legs and décolletage of one who smokes a cigarette. Talking, laughing, and putting their cracked, bare soles on the seats, the girls settle in across from Aliye and me. The cologne bearer comes around, and I am relieved that they know how to thank him in Turkish.

Presently the boys begin to sing in low tones. After about ten minutes, someone from the back of the bus comes up and complains to the driver. He looks at a pair of swarthy male passengers who then turn to me. Together the men tell me the singing is annoying peoplc in thc back of the bus; they want me to talk to the boys. I translate and the boys stop immediately, apologizing profusely. Not long after, the driver plays a cassette of a popular quarter-tone vocalist. Aliye sighs, "That's İbrahim Tatlıses [İbrahim Sweet Voice], my favorite."

It's mid-afternoon and the landscape with its dark, broken basalt radiates heat. Kurdish tribes-women and their herds provide interest between stretches of burned wheat fields. Resplendent in Lurex-shot skirts and silk headscarves, the women mind the sheep, who seem to graze on rock, so sparse is the vegetation now. But we pass one patch of chartreuse flora and see a score of blue wooden boxes—beehives—that a migratory apiarist has set down for the period of evanescent bloom.

In the distance, and then right beside the road, I count the summer tents, five there, a dozen here, and some solitaires. The tent-sides are drawn up, the black goat-hair fabric giving only shade against the sun. Reed lattices lashed to the tent-poles let the breezes through and provide privacy. Like shadow puppets, the inhabitants are silhouetted with their bundles of bedding and cooking utensils.

An hour west of Diyarbakır, Aliye gets off in her town of Siverek. I've learned a lot of my Turkish translating place-names on journeys like this, but Siverek eludes me and the small dictionary I carry as a linguistic talisman. Only half-seriously, I speculate that the name is a contraction of *sivrisinek*, which means mosquito. After Aliye has gone, I wish I'd asked her about the malaria, but perhaps it would have been for naught. If I'd not been with her, she might have eaten the raw *köfte* in Urfa....

I stretch out across the now-vacant seat. One of the men who was bothered by the singing smiles at me with a blaze of gold incisors. "Have you been to Diyarbakır before?" he asks.

"No," I say. He smiles again and shrugs.

Just outside Diyarbakır, we pass gargantuan radar dishes and neat barracks behind barbed wire. Far from the North Atlantic, this is a NATO post nonetheless. The not-so-friendly skies of Syria, Iraq, and Iran are close enough to enjoy the same weather that greets one here. The dry, clear golden light of this afternoon would sing "September" anywhere north of the Tropic of Cancer. We pull into the Diyarbakır bus station about five; I make a point of arriving in new places by daylight, the better to get my bearings. Within a minute, my luggage and I are in a taxi heading for the old city.

My hotel in Gaziantep has called ahead to make me a reservation, not in either of the two preferred hotels, which are full, but in a third that the taxi finds next to a barber shop in a tiny alley off the main street. Other foreigners with much professional photographic equipment are draped around the lobby. They look as if they've been waiting too long for something, and ridiculously, Dali's melting watches come to mind....

My room has been reserved, and I ask to see it. Basic Anatolian accommodations: blessedly hard twin beds, clean linens, and a layer of dust on everything else. On the sixth floor, the room overlooks litter of old wine bottles and papers on an adjaceant roof. I ask to see another room; this hotel is not full. The one across the hall is smaller, has a double bed, and faces east across a dingy airshaft. But it also looks out over the citadel walls to wheat fields which set off a black, square-sided minaret. There's a private bath with a tub that will never again be scrubbed clean and a pervasive quiet— all for less than seven dollars a night. I agree to take the room. There are no window screens; I wonder briefly about mosquitos—or larger creatures—that might find their way in.

The bellboy dials my phone to tell the reception staff to send up my bag. The dial falls off in his hand. The bag is delayed because the elevator is being fixed. I ask the boy if he speaks Kurdish. "Yes, we all do," he answers.

"Tell me the Kurdish for 'please'?" He struggles. "How about 'thank you'?"

Pause. "We don't really have the words in the same way as Turkish."

My suitcase arrives. The room is so tiny—about eight by nine feet, with a "foyer," about two feet deep—that I have to open the case beneath what serves as a dressing table. I call down to the desk for toilet paper, once something one didn't even expect in the East. Despite the broken dial, the message gets through.

I am tired and a nap is tempting, but so is the city at my feet. My *Guide Bleu* calls Diyarbakır *insolite*." (Eccentric, bizarre, with overtones of the unfathomable, it's the word M.F.K. Fisher chose to describe Marseille, a town I liked at first bite.)

I tie on a headscarf and hit the streets, and no mere mean streets, these. No, the main north-south thoroughfare is the *cardo maximus* from the city's Roman era. And this is the hour of the self-indulgent stroll, the promenade of pleasure and posturing that is practiced from Iberia to Palestine. That the Mediterranean *paseo* should also occur at the western edge of the Latin world, in, say, Valparaiso, is slight surprise. But here, in the boondocks of old Rome that were once the first line of defense against the Persian Empire, the persistence of custom provokes more thought. A few fair tourists, sunburned in their sleeveless shirts, stand out among the hennaed tresses, dark eyes, and moustaches of the ambling throng.

Pedestrians spill off the sidewalks onto the main streets. Parallel to the walks, trenches five feet deep are being dug to expose sewer pipes. Repairs, I assume. Laborers with heads wrapped in black and white *kefiyes* work their way through layers of the city. Doubtless they'll turn up things—coins, perhaps some of the stone seals Lawrence sought. (In Turkey, too, municipal improvements are repeatedly delayed or altogether thwarted by the inopportune discovery of CULTURE when the mayor and his constituents would settle for storm drains.) Shovels of dirt arc through the air. Rickety crossovers of broken pavement and boards are poised at strategic points. Tea servers and porters jockey for position amongst conversing men in baggy *şalvar* and slow-moving mounds of black veiling—women lingering before the illuminated displays of gold in the jewelers' windows.

One sound rises above the burble of Kurdish and Turkish: it is a delicate metallic "teka-teka-teka-teka-tek." Scattered throughout the crowds are licorice sherbet-sellers jangling copper cups on chains. Given the numbers of people, I am struck by the relative (and delightful) quiet, due to a paucity of motorized vehicles. Since prosperous Turkish cities are now locked in mortal combat with the internal combustion machine, one must take it as a negative measure of Diyarbakır's economy that the scent of evening bread is more evident than exhaust fumes.

Is it poverty or simply neglect that is expressed in the contemporary architecture of Diyarbakır?

Except for hotels and offices, most of the buildings have unstuccoed, haphazardly mortared brick walls. Compared to other Turkish towns in the late 1980's, there is very little reinforced concrete. I've already noted that my hotel room has no two planes parallel and that the exterior wall below my sill is crumbling. A traveller who has adopted a certain personal fatalism, I finger the blue glass evil-eye bead in my pocket. I know I am lodging on shaky ground, earthquake country.

For decades now, the accusations and insinuations have ricocheted between the capital of Ankara and the supposedly unruly eastern provinces. From the western camp with its suave bureaucrats, one hears that eastern Turkey is underdeveloped because of the stubborn ignorance of its people, who shun the social liberalism of the Europe-leaning western portion. In the east the view is, predictably, different: Ankara is slow to foster development there because even though the inhabitants are Turkish citizens and co-religionist Sunni Muslims, many are Kurds, not ethnic Turks. According to the prevailing opinion, Ankara fears the Kurds' numbers, variously estimated to be anywhere from four to ten million within the country's overall population of 55 million.

One sore point is substandard housing, blamed for high death tolls in devastating earthquakes which in the last two decades have struck Diyarbakır, Van, and other largely Kurdish provinces in the mountainous east. Most of the rural eastern Anatolian population lives in flat-roofed mud-brick houses, death-traps in a quake.

But another sort of upheaval has been an economic shot-in-the-arm for Turkey. To many who once supplemented their irregular incomes by smuggling spare parts for DeSotos and Chevrolets across slackly guarded southern borders, the Iran-Iraq war presented greater commercial opportunities. For the duration of the war, Turkey maintained its neutrality and allowed arms, food, and other goods to pass from Europe, on to Iran and Iraq. Many Turkish citizens, including Kurds, have made money in legitimate and illegitimate traffic with the warring states.

In the salons of Istanbul, anyone from the east—Kurd or not—is suspect until he has proven himself socially adroit, or rich. During my stay in Diyarbakır I learn that a very wealthy "Istanbul" family whose business supports a conspicuously lavish lifestyle in that city as well as in New York, is, in fact, not long out of Diyarbakır. As I look around the town, I see little evidence that they or others like them have been reinvesting in their home town.

Palpably different from any other metropolis in Turkey, Diyarbakır is intriguing. But how Turkish is it? Appearing in recorded history for at least four millenia, Diyarbakır, known in antiquity as Amida, has had a variety of rulers. In 297 A.D. one of Diocletian's lieutenants added it to Rome's real estate in Asia Minor. Roman engineers laid down the *cardo maximus* and supplemented existing fortifications. (The walls were extensively rebuilt later, in medieval times.) After Constantine's break with Rome, Amida was alternately lost and regained in battles between the Byzantines and Persians. It was the Byzantines who, in 639, lost Amida to the Arab clan of the Bakir, whose name was then applied to the settlement: the "place of Bakir." Subsequent rulers included other Arab, Mongol, Kurdish, Selcuk, and Turkmen dynasties. The city, which the Turks called Kara Amid (Black Amida, after the basalt walls) only became part of the Ottoman Turkish Empire in 1516.

But most cities in this part of the world have such checkered pasts. What, besides seventy-odd defense towers built into more than three miles of black walls, has kept this town apart and, well, *insolite*? In my tour brochure, I describe the city as Turco-Arab, so as not to embarrass my local travel agent or any of my other Turkish friends. Nonetheless, we all know it as the *de facto* capital of the Kurds. Recently arriving Kurdish refugees from Iran and Iraq have increased the Turkish government's sensitivity about the indigenous Anatolian Kurds, a large ethnic minority only partially assimilated into modern Turkish society. Tour guides are supposed to call the colorful Kurdish pastoralists "mountain Turks." No matter that the Kurds and their language are Indo-European, and that Xenophon, writing his *Anabasis*, described encounters with the Carduchians, a rugged people in eastern Anatolia that were probably ancestors of today's Kurds.

After the Persian campaigns and before their joyous arrival, in 400 B.C., on the coast of the Black Sea, where they cried "*Thalassa*!" Xenophon and the "Ten Thousand" were forced to march through hostile eastern Anatolia, via Mesopotamia. Abstaining from plunder, hoping for promises of safe conduct and permission to requisition food for their numbers, the Hellenes found that—

> "...the Carduchians neither gave ear when they called to them, nor showed any other friendly sign.... A party of the Carduchians made an attack...killing some and wounding others with stones and arrows... The Carduchians kept many watch-fires blazing in a circle on the mountains and kept each other in sight all round."

When what was left of the Hellenic mercenaries finally extricated themselves from this inhospitality, Xenophon assessed their experience thus:

> "...the last seven days spent traversing the country of the Carduchians had been one long continuous battle which had cost them more suffering than the whole of their troubles at the hands of the king and Tissaphernes put together.
>
> —*Anabasis* by Xenophon, circa 400 B.C.

Though the friction between modern Greece and Turkey is well known, Xenophon's cohorts had something in common with today's Turkish government: the same wary view of certain denizens of eastern Anatolia. The problem, for Ankara's officialdom, if not for the average citizen, is that the Kurds were here in Mesopotamia long before the Turks had stirred from the steppes of Central Asia. Atatürk's modern state of Turkey, forged in the 1920's from the filings of the Ottoman Empire, has not yet entirely amalgamated the ethnic diversity of the territory that comprises Turkey today. It may be that ethnic pluralism was better tolerated by the wheezing administration of the Sick Man of Europe than by a late twentieth-century republic clamoring for membership in the European Economic Community. Improvement of its human rights profile vis à vis the EEC members is widely supposed—by Turkish intellectuals and European Turkey-watchers—to be the chief motive behind the Turkish government's 1988 grant of asylum to some 60,000 Kurds fleeing chemical warfare attacks launched against them by the Baghdad government. There's a Turkish saying that Kurds fear neither man nor God. Yet clearly, the latest Kurdish refugees have been terrorized by something outside their people's long and difficult experience with the sovereign powers of the Middle East.

Though there was talk of fashioning an autonomous Kurdish state in the aftermath of Turkey's defeat in World War I, the Kurds—today inhabiting parts of Syria, Lebanon, Turkey, Iraq, Iran, Afghanistan, and the former Soviet Union—have never, in all their history, enjoyed a cohesive leadership.

Today it is illegal for Turkey's schools to teach the Kurdish language; the publication of Kurdish newspapers and books is likewise forbidden. (I have a copy of a Kurdish gazette published in Stockholm.) Any outsider measuring Turkey's political maturity by its tolerance of Kurdish culture will likely give Ankara a low grade, unless he looks at the current practices of Iran and Iraq, where Kurdish agitation for greater autonomy and cultural freedom has been met with more bitter repression. Battling each other, both Tehran and Baghdad have also been fighting their own Kurdish populations, who first saw the Iranian-Arab war as an open window for Kurdish aspirations.

When we bring our group here next May, what will my friend Selim, the erudite Istanbul tour guide with whom I regularly work, have to say about the "mountain Turks" of Diyarbakır, here on the Tigris plain?

We'll have to say something, because it's impossible to ignore the Iraqi Kurdish militia, the *peshmerge*, whose sartorial style brightens the town.

Tucked into fine, beige wool *şalvar*, the soldiers' khaki shirts bear the stars and bars of army rank. The *peshmerge* wrap their checked *kefiye*s into compact turbans and cinch their waists with intricate tapestry cummerbunds. Disarmed and disarming, these men cut figures that suggest something other than their provisional status. They may be refugees, but they look as if they own the place.

With my Nordic coloring, credit cards, and return air ticket, I can practice little more than political dilettantism here. The irony, admitted by my Turkish friends in Ankara and Istanbul, is that I, a foreigner, know the eastern provinces, their charms and their problems, far more intimately than they—which is not to say I shall ever really know them. Many an *İstanbullu* having more than a passing acquaintance with Paris, and more recently, the luxury resorts on Turkey's Aegean and Mediterranean coasts, has barely visited the central Anatolian capital of Ankara, let alone any settlement to the east. Yet Turks like my friends—with votes, money, and military clout—will ultimately determine what becomes of the inhabitants of eastern Turkey.

I am in Diyarbakır to see for myself how things are, as much as that's ever possible in the Orient, where there are always at least three levels of "reality": the way things are said to be, the way one sees them, and the way things actually are.

I make my way to the Ulu Cami, the Great Mosque, whose Selcuk inscription dates it to the late eleventh century, making it the oldest in Anatolia. On our tours we tend to focus on architecture, and I am anticipating a splendid building, only to find a depressing edifice, dark within and without. For me, this structure lacks the harmony of later mosques. Part basilica, part forum, with Syrian and Corinthian elements jumbled together, the assemblage is far from ecumenical. Rather, with its over-sized courtyard, it seems a stage-set for some nameless, corrupted faith. What spirit can soar surrounded by black basalt? I depart, leaving behind a small knot of teen-aged boys whose eagerness to practice their French fails to inspire me to linger any longer within the morose sanctuary.

According to my *Guide Bleu*, a few yards outside the mosque is a small Koranic school, the Zincirli Medrese. I ask a few people on the street and draw a blank. When I ask a group of boys, one of them is directed to lead me there. As we set off down an alley, I soon realize two things—that my limping guide is further crippled by a hunchback and that he has no idea where we are going. I find it strange that he has been attached to me. I give him a coin, bid him good evening, and retrace my steps. The *medrese* can wait, I decide; there's another mosque I'd like to visit. My map shows it deep inside a residential quarter, far from the main streets. I chance upon a scholarly-looking man, bearded and wearing the soberly tailored wool suit that seems to be *de rigueur* here (Western-style jacket and vest worn above voluminous *şalvar*). Placing my right hand over my heart, I greet him. "Peace be upon you."

"And upon you," he answers. I ask him the way to the mosque of Behram Paşa. "You should not go alone," he says calmly, "nor at dusk. Come back by day, and we'll send you with a child who knows the way."

I thank him for his concern. The situation is completely atypical. My experience in Turkey has always been that a single woman on a city street, though she may draw stares, is safe day or night. Still, I heed the advice and return to the fluorescent lights of the main drag and its now-familiar rhythm, the teka-teka-tek of the sherbet-sellers.

Like all the legions that have assaulted this land, tourists march on their stomachs. Thinking of my group next spring, I make my first forays into the Diyarbakır restaurant scene. Along the walls are illuminated signs that say "BAR" and "GAZINO." One establishment is named "DO SI DO," undoubtedly a nod to NATO's homesick American enlistees. I wonder if I'll have to make do with more traditional domains where a single woman attracts just as much attention.

Provincial Turkish restaurants customarily advertise the presence of an *aile salonu*, a family or women's section where mixed couples and women alone may sit without the untoward glances of men outside their own families. Such areas frequently bear a second notice which says, "bachelors may not enter." Though I've never seen it posted that *aile* are unwelcome, this evening I quickly discover that beverage service on an attractive vine-covered terrace atop a sixteenth-century caravanserai would be disrupted by my patronage.

Entering a travel agency selling "luxury" bus tickets to places like Mosul and Jiddah, I ask for advice on finding Diyarbakır's best food. One of the agents immediately escorts me to a brightly-lit eatery where I am presented and received—like an awaited guest.

With a flourish, I am seated by myself at a corner table beside the young proprietor who orchestrates the evening from a swivel chair behind the cash drawer. Light-skinned and with the aquiline nose of Sultan Süleyman himself, he has the incipient paunch of a successful restaurateur. And he has an apprentice—his plump little brother, twelvish, poised on an adjacaent sofa.

I explain my research mission. Oven-warm *pide* bread, cool *ayran*, and the house specialty—an assortment of lamb, chicken, hot green peppers, and tomatoes, all charcoal-grilled and wreathed with much refreshing flat-leaved parsley—appear quickly. So do a few flies, which I whisk away when they threaten my *ayran* glass. It's been a long time since I've seen flies in a Turkish indoor restaurant, and on my way back from the mosque, I've already noticed their numbers in the food markets.

Throughout my meal and between their calculations of diners' bills, the owner and his brother chat with me. I can comprehend only a portion of their conversations with clients, for they switch back and forth between Kurdish and Turkish. I'm quite sure that, by their coloration and features, my hosts are Turks, but to answer the question I compliment them on their bilinguality and ask what language they use at home. "Turkish" is their reply.

"But, of course, you need Kurdish for business."

"Oh, yes, of course."

Noticing a spiral staircase and an arrow indicating the presence of an upstairs *aile salonu*, I feel privileged indeed to have been permitted to remain below with conversation and entertainment, the bustle of an ongoing concern. I've been served enough meat for three people, and much to my chagrin, I, a Stateside champion of tofu, make my way through most of it. The bill, with coffee and a tip (which the head waiter pushes into a tea tin on the cashier's desk), is about three dollars. As I exit, the little brother douses my hands with cologne. Five people wish me good-night.

Back at my hotel, I leave my passport with the chipper receptionist who must register all guests with the police. The elevator is working, and I decide to trust it to deliver me to my floor, which it does. The night is dry, with no whine of mosquitoes. I leave the window open to the silence of the sparkling sky.

By five-thirty, dawn has outlined the far bank of the Tigris and my black minaret in watermelon pink. Melons are much on my mind, and I hope they'll share today's agenda with hotels and restaurants. A friend named Vassilios, a botanist working on melon cultivars in Australia, has heard of Diyarbakır's legendary melons—not only the hundred-pound watermelons fertilized with pigeon droppings, but also the orange, green, and white-fleshed varieties. I have been informally commissioned to ask questions, eat melons, and save seeds which I am to post to Australia. Too restless to make a good tourist, I welcome an assignment. This, no doubt, is why I organize tours and fill empty film canisters with seeds from luncheon fruits. Vassilios has shrewdly selected me for this very weakness.

But first, hotels. I visit five to inspect their restaurants, lobbies, rooms, and baths. I also note the courtesy or, in one case, indifference, of their reception staffs. Every hotel is better-appointed than my present lodgings, and tonight I could have a room in any of them, though none has friendlier employees. Reluctant to spend time in needless nomadism, I decide that for one more night I am content enough in my peaceful little cell.

At the Ministry of Tourism Office, I learn that the town's ethnographic, archeological, and Atatürk museums are closed for indefinite reasons and an indefinite period. But I also find a young engineering student eager to practice his English, and even more eager (Praise be to Allah!) to discuss melons for half an hour. This chance encounter gives me two long pages of notes for Vassilios—information about an orange winter melon which ripens in nets hung from household rafters and an inedible, grapefruit-sized melon grown solely for its power to perfume a room. Regrettably, the perfume-melon's season has just passed and the almost-annual Diyarbakır Watermelon Festival will not be held since the largest of this season weighed in at a paltry sixty-five pounds.... That this summer staffer at a sleepy tourist office should know so much suggests that the *Diyarbakırlı* take their melons with something besides a grain of salt...something more like a thick slice of briny sheep's milk cheese.

Out on the streets and in the covered produce markets, melons are heaped like cannonballs. I ask questions, jot down names. There are several I should like to taste, but I am a lone diner, a lone shopper. I cannot possibly eat, let alone carry back to the hotel, more than one melon. I select a small flower-scented, irregularly marked, orange one that weighs about two pounds. I learn its Turkish and Kurdish names. Can my Swiss Army knife and I, in my grubby yellow, green, and lavender tiled bathroom, really do justice to this cucurbit? In a flash of inspiration, I bear it back to the restaurant of last night's meal and dispatch it to the kitchen with instructions that someone slice it and save me the seeds.

I order my beloved *lahmacun*. Once again I am made comfortable at "my" table, and again the portion set before me is enormous. The owner's mother and other female relatives are introduced to me as they, in the conservative garb of pious city women—headscarves and raincoats worn regardless of weather—descend from the seclusion of the upstairs salon. They greet me warmly. Everyone in Diyarbakır uses the familiar form of address, like the French *tu*, and they are amused by my politely bookish Istanbul dialect. American or *İstanbullu*, either creature is a foreigner here.

The melon proves to be rather bland, despite the promise of it aroma. Nevertheless, I take the seeds back to my room and spread them out to dry on the windowsill.

This afternoon I plunge into the small bazaar in the hope of finding some of the sherbet-sellers' copper cups. There are no tourists on the metal-smiths' street, and no EuroPop ditties blare from the radio and cassette shops. The ambient tunes are all in minor keys. Everyone stares, but happily, I am years beyond finding this bothersome. Still, I am an outsider, so the asking price of the carved quail cage that enchants me is a week's salary for a ditchdigger. I examine some men's violet-striped pajama bottoms I might wear on another continent. A young boy, noting my interest in a pot of basil, gallantly plucks a sprig and presents it to me. He and his father ask my nationality, and I am pleased to tell them that although I am an American, Turkey is my second homeland. Big grins from the circle that gathers around us. I make my way to a stall selling prayer beads. The owner, pointing to a calendar picture of the Kaaba, proudly tells me he's gone four times to Mecca, where he's picked up some of the fine Indian and Pakistani beads in his stock.

I buy postcards of watermelons: watermelons in the foreground of the flowing Tigris, watermelons hoisted on the shoulders of folklorically-costumed women, and watermelons scooped out and filled with bewildered-looking toddlers.

The twentieth century has infiltrated Diyarbakır in curious ways. Heir to a respectable service, a boy squats on the sidewalk beside a bathroom scale with a liquid crystal display; his hand-lettered sign proclaims, "Your weight, scientifically, by computer!" In the twisting alleys of Turkish towns, the porter's profession is essential for transport of goods. Where narrowness precludes vehicles and the necessity for keen judgement knocks out dependence on donkeys, the *hamal* is still, in many areas, the only answer. Later, I draw aside to permit a *hamal* passage as he shoulders his load through the bazaar. His burden? Roped to the wool and straw saddle that protects his back is a computer monitor.

One of my Turcophilic American friends has vowed to leave his estate to endow an as-yet-nonexistent school of Turkish landscape architecture. Perhaps it should be founded here, in Mesopotamia, where Eve upset the applecart by offering Adam what ethnobotanists surmise was a pomegranate. Recognizing the preciousness of water here, one grasps why English lawns in the Middle East have enjoyed a transplant only marginally more successful than bacon and kippers for breakfast. Park planners seem determined to prolong the expulsion from Paradise, so partial are they to cement sidewalks over flowerbeds. Yet even for Turkey, municipal Diyarbakır is remarkable for its dearth of aesthetic planting. By the end of the day, I crave vegetation.

I want to see the Tigris, at sunset from the walls. Remembering the previous evening's admonitions, I negotiate for a taxi, though I'd rather walk. Arriving at the battlement said to possess the best view, the driver asks if I'd like him to accompany me. Since I've been anticipating a contemplative stroll along the wall, I ask him: "You mean, I *shouldn't* go up alone?"

"Uhh, no, it's only if you'd like me, uh, someone to— "

"Because something might happen?"

"No, nothing's likely to happen, *İnşallah*."

"I'd be pleased if you would join me," I say.

My driver does not bother to lock his car, but the sullen presence of a few young loiterers reclining on the stone stairway makes me grateful for the solicitousness he has shown me. The view from the wall *mérite un détour*, as Michelin would say. Garden plots, beginning at the base of the walls, carpet the slope for about a half mile before they meet the river. The mists of early dusk hang above the water and are beginning to spread over the peach and apricot orchards at the bottom of the valley. A few miles downstream, the arches of a graceful stone bridge vault across the river. Legend plants Eden near Diyarbakır, and a romantic with his back to the city's harsh basalt can believe anything.

"It's beautiful, isn't it?" says my driver.

This evening another restaurateur, Ziya, the handsome nephew of a friend of a friend, has asked me to join him for dinner at his restaurant, reputed to be Diyarbakır's best. Denim-clad couples, grandparents, and children sit amongst businessmen. No *aile salonu* here. I've only to ask a question and I'm hauled back to the kitchen to see the vast copper kettles holding a score of braised chickens or a pair of whole, stuffed lambs. Rice *pilav* steams in huge pots. We start with lemon-laced tripe soup. Then buttery lamb, sweet apricot compote, cucumbers with yogurt and mint all appear at once. Ziya springs up frequently to ring up a bill or run to the kitchen. He brings me a sample of his family's special seasoning: dried purple basil ground with black and red pepper. Ziya turns on the over-sized television at the front of the restaurant; his clientele ceases conversation and sits transfixed. He wants to know my choice in the upcoming U.S. presidential elections. Telling him I'm undecided, I say that either candidate is likely to be favorably disposed towards Turkey. Never forgetting Turkey's old quarrels, I hasten to add that Turks need not fear Michael Dukakis's Greek heritage. "You must believe he's an American first," I say.

"Certainly," says Ziya. "Those old fights are only for small people. Men in the eye of the world are beyond such little things." How I wish he were right! But what a pleasant surprise to hear his opinion, in a region where history would have us believe every altercation is doomed to echo for eternity.

He is dismayed that I have no children. "I've got three," he boasts, "and another on the way! You should have at least one!" In thc same generous tone, he urges me to share some semolina *helva*, slightly sweet, warm, and dusted with cinnamon. "I made this myself," he exclaims.

Though I've come in a taxi, Ziya offers to drive me back to my hotel via a famous shrine that he says I must see. A waiter helps him on with his suit jacket, and a friend tosses him the keys to a new Honda. We pull away from the curb at an alarming speed, and are waved through a police check-point. In the East it is said that a guest is a captive of the whole quarter.... Hospitality is hospitality, but I am relieved that the shrine is locked up for the night. Hoping to keep the evening on a genteel level, I ask Ziya to drop me off at the hotel. He seems genuinely disappointed that I am not more curious about *la vie nocturne* of Diyarbakır-sur-Tigre.... But with good humor, he backs down the alley that dead-ends at my hotel. As I thank him for his kindness, we shake hands. "We'll see you back here, in the spring," he says. "*İnşallah*, with your husband, too!"

On my last morning in Diyarbakır, I plan once more to find the hidden mosque of Behram Paşa. Purposely, I go by secondary streets until my way is blocked by a truck filled high with long, glossy violet eggplants. On top of the heap are seven boys engaged in hurling them down, like so much firewood, to the front porch of a shop painted turquoise. A voluptous scene!

The neighborhood seems benign, but as a last caution, I stop at a pharmacy to ask the way, and am told that the mosque is just ahead. "Will I have problems if I go alone?" The pharmacist seems surprised by the question.

"Why, no. But if you like, I'll send my assistant with you."

It is a bright morning and I decline the offer, preferring to proceed on my own. Behram Paşa's mosque is at once completely different from the hulking mass of the Ulu Cami. Drawn to the airy domed portico I can see through the bars of the fence around the compound, I am frustrated to find all the gates to the courtyard locked. A boy about fourteen tends one gate but refuses me entry. Other boys on the street gather around us, and two women with whom I've just exchanged *selams* are standing by. Then a young man with a five-day beard intervenes, asking the boy to unlock the gate. The boy refuses again. I explain that I'm a student, an admirer of Islamic architecture. More petulant refusal.

As a last resort, I say to him, "Look, Turkey is my home, too." And then stretching the truth, I let him have the line I've long held in reserve: "I'm not a tourist, I live here." Which, in a manner of speaking, I do.

"You see, now open up for her," orders the unshaven youth. Keys materialize and at least I'm able to admire the building from the front and sides. But the keys to the mosque itself are in other hands; the great front door is kept locked, except at prayer times. "Because of children. They throw rocks, break things," says my supporter.

I peer through the windows at walls of fine red, white, and cobalt İznik tiles that are definitely worth protecting. A locked mosque usually indicates a lean endowment, insufficient to support a full-time attendant. But it strikes me as peculiar that, in a close residential quarter, where everyone knows what everyone else is up to, a mosque could be imperilled by the children of the families it serves. For my tour next year, I make a note that I should come to Behram Paşa a little before the group, in order to find someone more likely to let us enter.

After leaving the mosque, I wander on my own, deeper into the city and find extraordinary designs ornamenting two-storey basalt houses. White stone has been finely cut and inlaid into the façades to depict vines, trees, birds, crescent moons, and beaming suns. I suspect that these are—or were—Armenian or Assyrian Christian houses from before the turn of the century, before the social eviscerations that stained this corner of the world.

An elderly Kurdish woman sitting in her doorway asks if I am looking for "the church." Though I am simply exploring, I am willing to follow the child she has lead me to a locked iron door. Before skipping back to her playmates, the girl bangs hard on the door and tells me someone will come. The door is opened and I enter a scene so unexpectedly lovely that I hear myself give a little gasp of delight.

I am in sunny courtyard, with one of the "inlaid" stone houses as a backdrop. The door and window frames are painted brilliant blue, like the summer sleeping platforms outdoors before the house. Closer to me is a stone well festooned with magenta and blue morning-glories. Swags of drying eggplants, green and red peppers, and yellow squash are garlanded about the courtyard like holiday lights. To the right is a church. (By now I've dug out my *Guide Bleu* and read the brief note that says it is Syrian Orthodox, and that portions of this complex may date from the fifth century.)

Inside are wooden pews, an altar, candles, and the lingering scent of incense so mnemonic of Eastern Christianity. There's a remarkable altar curtain of block-printed and hand-painted cotton, which I ask the young attendant to spread for me; it features a rooster (the cock that crowed three times before Peter denied Jesus) alongside the Crucifixion.

That all this should survive here amazes me. I stuff a bill into the collection box and talk with the attendant. His family lives in the pretty house. He is sixteen, out of school because he failed the lycée entrance examinations. Falus ("Like Paul," he says) knows Kurdish and is studying English on his own. His Turkish is good and he says his family, who look after the church property, speak Assyrian at home. I ask if I might come back with some Americans next May. He says he would be pleased and gives me his phone number.

"Are there still Armenians in Diyarbakır?" I ask.

"Yes, five families in this quarter."

"Only five?"

"Nearby, yes, but I don't know about the other neighborhoods."

"And Assyrians, like your family?"

"These people next door to the church are Assyrian." Falus leads me across his courtyard and through an arch to another dwelling. A very strong and sweet smell suffuses this yard: red pepper paste in broad, shallow pans sits concentrating in the sun. In the shade a woman and her daughter, both in patched, faded calico work clothes, sit coring peppers and cranking them through a food mill. The pepper pulp has dyed their hands a gory red. Falus leaves us and we converse about the peppers and their kitchen use.

"Did you come alone to Diyarbakır?" the woman asks.

"Yes, I did."

"This is no place to be alone," she says, shaking her head. "You are English?"

"American."

"From what part?"

"Between New York and Boston."

"We know someone in Chicago."

I don't tell her that I'd rather be alone in Diyarbakır than in Chicago.

I have one more stop before I must return to collect my melon seeds and check out of the hotel. When I reach the courtyard of the mosque of Melek Ahmet Paşa, it too is locked. I find a boy to look for the muezzin, who has the key. After about ten minutes, the muezzin and I are within the mosque, which is built above a complex of shops whose rent still helps support the religious institution. My chief interests here are the revetments of İznik tiles, second-rate ones, except for nearly hidden stairway panels whose abstract designs are unlike any other Turkish ceramics I know; a pleasant discovery. The cheerful muezzin proudly points out a tired Persian carpet donated to the mosque some years ago. Upon leaving, I mention my surprise that most of his city's mosques seem to be locked between prayer times. He, too, cites vandalism by "children."

There is more to this excuse than I can discern on my first visit, more to the cautions voiced for my well-being on certain streets. Though not completely ignorant of the city's old feuds, I can only guess at what animosities persist. Is Diyarbakır *insolite* or just insolent? There are also walls *within* this city, intangible walls as enduring as the stone ramparts that rise above the Tigris. I hand the muezzin the same sum I gave to the Syrian church. "Oh, you don't have to do that," he says waving away the note.

Imagining the addition of a pomegranate or rosebush to Melek Ahmet Pasa's foundation (which, in defiance of the local indifference to decorative flora, already supports a tree and a vine-covered trellis), I press the money against the muezzin's palm. "Let it help maintain the mosque," I say.

"For the mosque, then," he answers with a smile.

A long day's drive northwest of here, beyond the sources of the Euphrates, Julius Caesar briefly departed from practice, and with his "*Veni, vidi, vici,*" managed to speak of himself in the first person. But Ceasar never got this far, and two and a half days in

Diyarbakır are enough to convince me that this is a town one comes to see, but not to conquer. It must be met on its own terms.

Maybe not elsewhere in Turkey, but in Diyarbakır I have to admit: I am a tourist. And I'll be back.

14

Talismans

"Le superflu, chose très nécessaire."

—*Le Mondaine* by Voltaire, 1736

Even when I am far from this region with which I have become so inextricably involved, it commands my attention and comprises an ever-increasing measure of my existence. The arithmetic is irrefutable: I first went to Istanbul when I was eighteen, and my years have more than doubled since I gingerly entered Turkey's embrace.

Early on I acquired the carpets, horse trappings, beaten copper plates, and tinkling silver necklaces that beguile so many travellers there. Because selling such commodities funded my Turkish sojourns, I could easily justify their initial purchase—and eventual sale. I did not grieve upon parting with my favorite rugs, for I was compelled to see them as but a means to an end. Without an independent income, I had to choose between "having" and "doing," and I do not regret the choice I made. While accumulating experiences that can never be knocked down on any auction block, I became a temporary custodian (at times, even a curator) of wonderful things. Of course, not all I bought found a buyer. Because some of the finer (and costlier) objects were also among the more outlandish, I continue to enjoy those that have yet to arouse any of my customers to the point of purchase. But even more than the precious poundage of a nielloed silver belt or the pristine colors of a sixteen-foot Konya kilim, I treasure objects whose Turkishness is evocative rather than exclamatory, items whose virtue lies not in their substance, but in what they can conjure.

When considering any people's art and culture, I find the filings and shavings, the dust swept under the rug or through the floorboards, at least as interesting as the more monumental themes. A feather, a pebble, a cotton scarf, a wooden spoon—circumstances can transmute the inconsequential into formidable and priceless talismans.

How many times have I been cheered upon finding a sprig of myrtle (sacred to Aphrodite) or a meadow rose pressed dry between the pages of a guidebook, where months or years ago it marked a passage? Even if they've lost their fragrance, those are chance and happy findings, like the absent-minded leavings of a lover.

"And, strange to tell, among that Earthen Lot
Some could articulate, while others not..."

—*The Rubaiyat of Omar Khayyam* by Edward Fitzgerald

Shards.

Worn incisors in an aching jaw, pottery fragments from eroded civilizations lie imbedded in ancient earth. Where literacy is not a common legacy, oral histories ensure that recollection retains its bite and that memory is far sharper than any triangle of faience idly plucked from hallowed or cursed ground. Time and scouring sand smooth jagged edges of broken bowls more quickly than they heal hearts. But to an alien, the tales are intoned by the iridescent lip of a tear vial, a Roman child's blue glass bangle, and terra cotta amphora handles. And are these discarded melon rinds? No, just the green wedges of everyday glazed wares forever shattered, too mundane to warrant repair. Heaped on my kitchen counter, where I see them a dozen times each day, repose turquoise fragments I picked up near the Syrian border in the ruins of the Great Mosque at Harran. I give little thought to the vessels they once formed, but think often of Harran in Mesopotamia—where the old houses are domed like beehives, and where the *muhtar*, the village headman, lacking beans for the requisite Arab offering of coffee, poured us instant Nescafé, triple-strength, from his traditional beaked brass pot. The proverb says "a cup of coffee is worth forty years of friendship."

> "...the aspers, the small silver coins which were the standard currency of Turkish countries...were melted down and reissued with a gradually increasing proportion of copper—and as thinner coins: they were as light as the leaves of the almond tree and as worthless as drops of dew.'

—commentary on inflation by an unnamed
16th-century Turkish historian;
The Mediterranean, Vol. II, by Fernand Braudel (1966)

Coins, too, but not antiquities.

My biscuit-tin hoard of vanishing "croutons of the realm"† contains nothing struck before 1950. The world over, good coins are the casualties of inflation. When I first came in 1971, the exchange rate was twelve and a half Turkish lira to the U.S. dollar...now it is over seven thousand. Each lira is divided into 100 *kuruş*, and (strictly in theory these days) each *kuruş* is comprised of 100 *para*. It's been years since there were five and ten-*kuruş* pieces in circulation. Following the extinction of the single lira, the smallest denomination one is apt to see is the bantamweight ten-lira. The old lira were heavy and solid, and a day's worth of *dolmuş* fares could wear out a pocket, even though they fell short of the mimimum tip for a ten-block Manhattan taxi ride. New lira are hollow aluminum, almost as light as foil gum wrappers. My favorite piece from the old coinage was worth twenty-five *kuruş* and bore a woman in tribal headdress. The coin has vanished from circulation, but not its model, a gentle ethnographer and costume collector, the only monetary personage with whom I have ever shaken hands. On

†A felicitous phrase coined by Walter Denny.

the coin, as in real life, she wears her blond hair braided. Hers is a traditional coiffure—classically elegant, charming, reassuring, but incapable of stabilizing a currency. Heads, we lose.

What else? Paper.

I keep (as place-markers for cookbooks) all the "no pork" cards that accompany my airline meals in the Middle East; they feature an "X" superimposed over the silhouette of a pig. Then there is stationery: notepads and letterheads of sinuous calligraphy. Are the Turks attempting to recapture the romantic grace of Ottoman script and incorporate it into the workaday legibility of the Roman alphabet Atatürk forced upon them for their own good?

I have yet to learn which academic institution is responsible for the prevailing harum-scarum school of hotel graphics, exemplified by fonts whose undulant letters would conform to the curves of a cabaret dancer. Do any Turkish designers know of the ad-man's typeface called "Shish-Kabob," preferred print for American high-school programs of *Kismet* and packages of instant *tabbouleh*?

And then there are Turkish laundry tags, unobtrusively ironed inside waistbands and seams; they adhere for years, and outlast the clothing they once identified. Though I've never fancied luggage pasted with resort stickers, the wrong sides of my favorite garments bear the numbers of rooms happily occupied, records of my provisional homes.

All this finds its way into the traveller's suitcase, and thus his life. Packed up along with unmistakably Turkish-smelling soaps and the sewing kits whose extra buttons I'll never use are the plastic sacks printed in four languages with the warning, "THIS BAG IS NOT A TOY." What neurotic nostalgia prevents one from discarding things designed to be disposible? Mnemonic merit is independent of intrinsic value. So, a seventeen year-old plastic laundry bag from Room 303 at the moribund Commodore Hotel in Beirut compels me to write of vitality elsewhere.

"Happy the man who could search out the causes of things."
—*Georgics* I, Virgil (70-19 B.C.)

The swordsmiths, the gem-setters, and the embroiderers who created the treasures of Topkapı are dead and nameless. The poets, along with the calligraphers and miniature painters who glorified their words, have faired slightly better. At least we know a few of those by their brush and pen names, romantic sobriquets that only contribute to the enigma of the men behind them. *Nigari*, the chosen name of one seventeenth-century miniature master, itself means "embellished." Working for the glory of Allah alone or a state claiming His sanctions, the names of few Islamic artists have enjoyed the immortality of their works or the patrons who commissioned them.

With centuries of anonymous art behind him, the contemporary Turk's enthusiasm for establishing individual identity is a striking and often amusing departure from historic precedent.

The Turkish bakers at any blue-painted *ekmek fabrikası* (literally, "bread factory," although a bakery is usually a one-oven operation with two or three employees) are justifiably proud of their bread, which is the foundation of every Turkish meal. (Evliya Çelebi praises bakers as "those pillars of the faith.") Smaller than fortune cookie messages, tiny paper labels bearing a bakery's name and telephone number (if there is one) are slapped onto the bottoms of the dense, fragrant loaves. Clinging tenaciously, the labels carry their advertising to the tables at every social stratum, for thanks to government subsidies, every Turk can afford to buy this superior bread fresh each day. Because it is often easier to eat the labels than to peel them off, it is fortunate that there are no rumors of their discomfitting any diner. Whether or not the labels are digestible is a less provocative question than why the average Turkish consumer might *want* a bakery's phone number. (Open every day, bakeries are numerous, their production copious, and the variety of their goods limited. One simply stops and buys bread.) The suspicion is that the baker proclaims his number for another reason. The sheer presence of a telephone conveys a certain standing and dignity by suggesting that he knows the right people, i.e. others with telephones they use to call him. (Is it the photographers or the enterprising young rug dealers, pop musicians, and politicians who decide that their publicity photos should depict them cradling telephone receivers?) Whatever the case, the bakers like to keep pace.

Like the minute black seeds of *Nigella sativa* (blue-flowered Love-in-a-Mist) occasionally sprinkled on the tops of loaves, the paper labels impart one more subtle flavor to the bakers' creations. The staff of life reflects the very existence it sustains.

Turkish genius is well-represented in Portugal's newest mosque, in Lisbon. For the building's embellishment, Muslim communities throughout the world have donated examples of their artisans' skills. Turkey's gift has pride of place in the main prayer niche, the *mihrab*, faced with lovely floral tiles in the Ottoman style. If one does not already recognize them as the distinctive ceramics of Kütahya, the craftsman's name and phone number, painted among the leaves and blossoms, leave no doubt. Only the international dialling codes are lacking.

With Turkey's explosion of private enterprise and the proliferation of electronic communication, telex codes have already ceased to be the last word in label chic. Now the insoles of better-made shoes sport not only manufacturers' names, but also their fax numbers. The idea that the footwear phone numbers are printed purely for their cabalistic powers is supported by the complete absence of physical addresses. What other use have such numbers in Istanbul, where in the middle of a conversation, private lines may become party lines and the numerical exchanges have been altered *en masse* at least four times in the last decade?

Since the 1920's when Atatürk decreed that Turkey adopt the Latin alphabet, three generations have matured, but this is still a people newly literate. They define themselves with labels. The interlocking Gucci "g's" and "I LOVE NEW YORK" T-shirts serve as the cyphers and banners of this age. There is a reverence for print, no matter where it falls.

Entranced by the efficacy of their own advertising, Turkish banks regard any surface as potential proclamation space. Their logos and slogans compete on hotel showercaps and complimentary tubes of shampoo.

It is no mere love of things Western that imbues Adidas, Pierre Cardin, and Revlon with cachet—it is as much a love of labels. In the back alleys of Stamboul, there are tiny workshops (*atölye* they call them in transmogrified French) where bogus Wrangler and Levi patches are manufactured for locally produced blue jeans.

A Turkish friend on her first trip to the States surveys the wares of Bloomingdale's and Saks Fifth Avenue. After floors of clothing, accessories, and home furnishings, she asks me, in English, "Who is Designer?" She understands Givenchy, but how do I explain that the aesthetic forces behind "designer Kleenex" and Haitian jeans with phony Italian names are as anonymous as the illuminators of the sultans' gilt manuscripts?

To protect himself, a shopkeeper will make an "X" on the reverse side of his business card before he hands it over. In Turkey, anyone receiving a card so marked knows that its bearer is not the one named on the card. One's good name is worth everything, and precautions are taken to guard it and see that its use is authorized.

I treasure the card presented to me years ago in Aksaray. It reads:

> **MEHMET YILMAZ**
> **Farmer**

And so, the cross-pollination of East and West increases the vegetation in our gardens of delight.

Working Notes

TOUCH

Textures of bath mitts, from coarse silk to wool gabardine to the near-Brillo pad of black goat-hair; pumice stones on street-calloused heels.

Fingernails, ragged from opening pistachio shells.

Brittle newsprint that yellows in fifteen minutes of sunlight.

Fleece of new lambs; slippery satin bridal quilts.

Plumes of dill-weed; salt-wrinkled black olives glistening with oil.

Cool İznik tiles with tomato-red pigment in relief, like drops of ketchup; Persian verses deeply carved on marble tombstones.

SCENT

Rain—laying dust and diesel particles on cement sidewalks; coal smoke in fog; the tanneries of Yedikule; *rakı*; ox-dung fires.

Samanpazarı: lentils, henna, and naphthalene; cubes of olive oil soap; copper-tinning; tarnished silver; horses.

Damp, musty mosque carpets.

Dervishes perspiring.

Artemisia, its fragrance released by the hot marble of a toppled column.

Fresh fish and gasoline; citrus peels, parsley, pickles, roasting kebabs; *pastırma* cured with garlic and fenugreek; Ramazan *pide* late afternoon; roasting chickpeas; Bursa peaches.

The "acceptable" lemon colognes: Pereja and Boğaziçi; cheap scents colored like liqueurs.

Alcohol and cotton balls in pharmacies; Omo laundry detergent.

May nights drowned by Russian olive and linden in bloom; privet in June.

SOUND

Foghorns and ferry whistles; feet on the gangplanks at rush hour.

Startled pigeons at Yeni Cami.

Street vendors' cries; *Boza*! *Eskici*! *Süt*! *Enginar*![†]

Brake-screeching vehicles, klaxons, jingling harnesses; cars going over the speed bumps at the Hilton; trains inching across the Plateau.

[†]Millet beer! Rag and bone man! Milk! Artichokes!

Muezzins; wedding, circumcision, and Janissary bands; bagpipes, finger-cymbals, *dolmuş* radios.

Quavering echoes of welcome from nightclub microphones: "*Hoş-hoşhoş gel-gelgeldiniz....*"

Sheep bells, cicadas, Toros winds in the pines.

Eerie song of the Egyptian nightjar, like breath blown over an empty bottle.

TASTE

Hoofy white cheese; yeasty warm Tekel beer; salted purple carrot juice; smokey *ayran* at the Cihanbeyli bus stop; bitter tea and breakfast olives; slightly burnt sesame on *simit*; syrup-drenched pastry with unsweetened coffee; cornelian cherry and pomegranate juices; bergamot-scented *helva*; Kızılay mineral water; dried mackerel and sweet cucumbers; watermelons; *rakı* and salted chick peas; fresh pistachios in Antep; *roka* greens; dark Buzbağ wine; *İskender* kebab; mealy yellow potatoes; apricots with *kaymak*; caramel "Roma-style" ice cream in Yeşilköy; baked quinces and pumpkin with walnuts; rose-petal jam and nigella seeds on bread; *lokum*, black radishes, fresh figs, grilled cow corn, hazelnut butter, Thracian rice, *bulgur*, yogurt with a skin of yellow cream....

Sandoz 1000 mg. vitamin C tablets, artifical orange flavor. Dropped in a glass of water, they fizz...our tonic against Ankara's cold winter smog.

SIGHT

Back-lit arabesque panels on the Galata Bridge; the curved shore at Bebek and the Egyptian summer residence; mammary domes of the Otel Splendid on Büyükada; Ottoman stone bird houses; iron window grates of Roxelana's tomb.

On the sidewalks: sellers of plastic combs, postcards, and nail-clippers.

Against Topkapı illuminated for night: ferries dancing in the Golden Horn.

Heavy-headed dowager lilacs and blowsy roses; lavender Judas trees on the grey slopes of Rumeli Hisarı; blue-stemmed thistles; lavender opium poppies.

Rainbow plumage of migrating Abyssinian rollers.

Herds of grey speckled horses on the steppe near Ani.

Women with hair rinsed a coppery purple tone actually known as "eggplant;" long lacquered toe-nails; schoolroom images of Atatürk; eight year-olds with flat skulls and creased foreheads.

Sunset on the Bosphorus: A Saudi man in white and a quartet of women in sheer black veiling wave to us from their boat. In response, we toss them a bouquet of miniature carnations; they drift in the wake of our craft.

The Salt Lake in July, seven in the evening: lens at F 22, diamond glare. Emerald crater lake atop Nemrut Dağı. Ararat above the clouds; charcoal sky and lopsided moon over Armenia.

Striped *hamam* towels drying on the roofs, like lines of signal flags.

Crocheted amulets sewn to the underwear of children going away to school.

Over doorways and hotel reception desks; in elevators; on gold charm bracelets and orlon baby sweaters; hung from horse bridles, keyrings, rearview mirrors, and exhaust pipes— BLUE BEADS.

A Turkish Glossary

ABLA—older sister; term of respect, like "ma'am."

AFİYET OLSUN—"bon appetit," said before, after, and during a repast.

AĞA—lord, master; older brother.

AİLE SALONU—(lit., "family or women's salon") arca of a restaurant or other public place set aside for mixed groups.

ALLAH—Muslim name for God.

ALLAHA İSMARLADIK—(lit., "we have commended you to God") "good-bye," said by those departing

AŞURE—sweet pudding of wheat kernels, chick peas, beans, nuts, and dried fruit; it is made to commemorate the martydom of Hüseyin.

ATATÜRK—(lit., "Father Turk") Mustafa Kemal Paşa, founder and first president (1922-38) of the Turkish Republic.

AYRAN—yogurt beaten with equal parts of water and served as a cool drink.

BAHARAT—spices; BAHARATÇI—spice merchant.

BAKLAVA—(see YUFKA) fine pastry leaves buttered and layered with ground nuts; usually drenched in a sugar syrup, though sometimes left "dry."

BAYRAM—a holiday, esp. KURBAN BAYRAMI, commemorating Abraham's sacrifice of a ram in place of his son.

BEBEK—attractive community on the European side of the Bosphorus. When Constantinople was the capital of the Empire, several embassies had summer residences there.

BEY—gentleman; "sir" when used after a first name. Ex: Kenan Bey

BİT—a flea; BİT PAZARI—second-hand market.

BÖREK—any of various savory YUFKA pastries filled with meat or cheese.

BOSPHORUS—(Turkish: Bosfor or Boğaziçi, lit., "inside the throat") strait between European and Asian Istanbul; it connects the Black Sea with the Sea of Marmara.

BOZA—thick, non-alcoholic beverage made from fermented millet.

BULGUR—cracked, parboiled wheat, the staple starch in Anatolia; most often steamed and served as a PİLAV.

BURMA—pistachio-filled coils of YUFKA in sugar syrup.

BÜYÜKADA—(also known as Prinkipo) the largest of the Princes' Islands in the Sea of Marmara and a popular summer resort for Istanbul's residents.

CAMİ—mosque; possessive form is CAMİİ.

ÇARŞI—a market or shopping area;
KAPALI ÇARŞI—Istanbul's Covered Bazaar.

ÇELEBİ—refined, well-bred, educated; an honorific used by dervishes.

ÇINAR—European sycamore or plane tree; *Platanus orientalis.*

ÇİNTAMANİ—any of the many Turkic decorative patterns based on combinations of wavy lines and/or spheres.

DAĞ—mountain; possessive form is DAĞI.

DOLMA—a hollow vegetable or leaf stuffed with rice and/or meat.

DOLMUŞ—a jitney taxi or mini-bus stuffed with passengers.

DÖNER—meat and fat layered together and roasted on a large revolving vertical spit.

EFENDİ—(also EFFENDİ) gentleman; a title of respect.

EKMEK—bread.

ELLİK—claw-like wooden finger-protectors worn by peasants scything grain.

EVLİYA—lit. "the saints" in Arabic.

EYGAL—(Arabic) heavy cord worn to keep a KEFİYE (head-cloth) in place.

EZAN—the call to prayer, given by a muezzin from the minaret of a mosque.

FISTIK—a pistachio; used to describe something easily accomplished ("a piece of cake") or to mean "cute," "pretty," or "sexy."

GALATA—European Christians' quarter on the north slope above the GOLDEN HORN.

GOLDEN HORN—(Turkish: Haliç) inlet of the Bosphorus separating GALATA from STAMBOUL.

HAL—(transliteration of the French *halle*) a large, covered produce market.

HAMAL—a porter.

HAMAM—a Turkish bath-house.

HAN—a caravanserai or provincial post-house for travelling merchants and their animals; an urban warehouse for homogenous groups of merchants such as wholesalers of carpets, grain, or honey.

HANIM—lady; wife; respectful title following a woman's name.

HELVA—any of numerous sweet pastes prepared with cereals, sesame, or nuts mixed with oil, sugar, and flavoring extracts.

HOCA—a Muslim preacher; a teacher.

HOŞ GELDİNİZ—"Welcome!"

HÖYÜK—tumulus; small hill created by centuries of settlement.

İNŞALLAH—(Arabic) "If God wills" or "Let's hope so"; also said by non-Muslims.

KADAYIF—any of several syrup-soaked pastries, especially one whose dough resembles shredded wheat.

KALE—castle; fortress.

KAŞIK—spoon.

KATMER—pistachio and semolina-filled breakfast pastry, a specialty of Gaziantep.

KAYMAK—clotted cream; often used figuratively to describe a pretty woman.

KEBAB—(also KEBAP) roasted or grilled meat.

KEDİ—cat.

KEFİYE—(Arabic) traditional head-cloth worn by men in Kurdish and Arab areas.

KEKİK—thyme, marjoram, or oregano; (colloquial) any aromatic wild herb.

KEYİF—(from Arabic; Durrell writes KAYF) sense of pleasure and well-being.

KİLİMs—traditional Mideastern and Balkan folk weavings employed as rugs, wall-hangings, coverlets, storage sacks, and animal trappings—Usually tapestry-woven, they are without a nap and may be reversible.

KISMET—destiny, fate, fortune.

KÖFTE—raw or cooked balls of ground meat flavored with herbs and spices.

KÖPEK—dog.

KÜLLİYE—complex of buildings (shops, baths, schools) adjacent to a mosque.

LAHMACUN—a pliable "pizza": rounds of dough thinly spread with ground meat, onions, peppers, and tomatoes, then quickly baked in a hot oven.

LEBLEBİ—roasted chickpeas nibbled with drinks.

LOKUM—candy made with cornstarch and sugar syrup; known as Turkish Delight.

MANTI—meat-filled dough, poached and served hot with yogurt and butter.

MAŞALLAH—exclamation: "May God Bless!" also used as "Wonderful!"

MEHMET—a male name; used, like "Johnny," to refer to a low-ranking soldier.

MEVLEVİ—members of the sect following the teachings of Celâlettin Rumi.

MEZE—appetizers, especially those served with alcoholic beverages.

MİHRAB—(also MİHRAP) architectural niche indicating the direction of Mecca.

MUHABBET—love; friendly affection.

MUHTAR—a village headman.

NARGİLE—a water-pipe, hookah, hubble-bubble.

NATIR—masseuse in a Turkish bath.

PASTIRMA—Turkish pastrami; pressed, air-dried meat cured with salt, garlic, cumin, and fenugreek.

PAŞA—pasha; highest rank of Ottoman civil and military officials; honorific for a male servant; endearment for a male child.

PAZAR—a bazaar; Sunday.

PEYNİR—cheese.

PİDE—any of various flat breads made with leavened dough.

PİLAV—rice or BULGUR fried in butter or oil, then boiled and/or steamed.

RAKI—arak; potent, colorless spirit usually distilled from grain and flavored with anise; it becomes cloudy when mixed with ice or water.

RAMAZAN—ninth month of the Islamic lunar calendar when the pious fast between dawn and sunset; it falls approximately eleven days earlier each year.

ROKA—arugula, rocket, roquette; the salad green *Eruca sativa*.

RUMELİ—European Turkey; RUMELİ HİSARI—15th-century fortress on the European shore of the Bosphorus; the residential district around the fortress.

SELAM ALEYKUM—Muslim greeting, "Peace be upon you." ALEYKUM SELAM is the reply.

SELCUKS—Turkish dynasty that ruled much of central and eastern Anatolia (A.D. 1071-1283) from their capital, Konya.

SİMİT—rings of sesame-sprinkled bread peddled by SİMİTÇİ, street-vendors.

STAMBOUL—old name for the quarter south of the GOLDEN HORN; it contains Istanbul's major Byzantine and Ottoman monuments.

SU—water.

SUFİ—(also Sofi; lit. "clothed in wool") a Muslim mystic; a dervish.

SÜLEYMAN I—Sultan known as "The Magnificent." His reign (1520-66) saw the Ottoman Empire at the zenith of its power and artistic accomplishment.

ŞARAP—wine.

ŞALVAR—baggy trousers worn throughout Muslim countries by both men and women.

TAMAM—the end; expression used to mean "okay" or "it's finished."

TEKKE—a dervish lodge or convent.

TİFTİK—fine white wool from the Angora goat.

YALI—a waterfront home, especially one of the large, wooden 18th or 19th-century houses whose balconies and intricate gingerbread grace the upper Bosphorus.

YASAK—forbidden.

YASAK BÖLGE—forbidden zone.

YAYLA—mountain pastures grazed in warm weather

YERLİ—local, indigenous, native.

YEŞİLKÖY—an Istanbul suburb on the European shore of the Sea of Marmara. Site of the city's domestic and international airports, its name means "green village."

YUFKA—paper-thin sheets of hand-rolled dough used in sweet or savory pastry.

ZEYBEK—swashbuckling young man from southwestern Anatolia; a flamboyant dance performed by men of that region.

A Brief and Idiosyncratic Bibliography

Atil, Esin; *THE AGE OF SULEYMAN THE MAGNIFICENT*; National Gallery of Art; Washington, D.C., 1987.

Birge, John Kingsly; *THE BEKTASHI ORDER OF DERVISHES*; Luzac & Co. (London) with Hartford Seminary Press; Hartford, Connecticut, 1937.

Braudel, Fernand; *THE MEDITERRANEAN AND THE MEDITERRANEAN WORLD IN THE AGE OF PHILIP II*; trans. by Sian Reynolds; Harper & Row; New York, 1972.

Efendi, Evliya (a.k.a. Evliya Çelebi); *NARRATIVE OF TRAVELS IN EUROPE, ASIA, AND AFRICA* (a.k.a. *SEYAHATNAME*); written in the 17th century; translation from Ottoman Turkish by Joseph Von Hammer, 1834; Johnson Reprint Corporation; New York, 1968.

Freely, John; *Blue Guide ISTANBUL*; W.W. Norton & Co.; New York, 1983. Includes virtually all of *STROLLING THROUGH ISTANBUL* (see below).

Halman, Talat Sait (editor); *CONTEMPORARY TURKISH LITERATURE*; Associated University Presses, Inc.; East Brunswick, New Jersey, 1982.

Kelly, Laurence (editor); *ISTANBUL, A TRAVELLER'S COMPANION*; Atheneum; New York, 1987.

Kinross, Lord; *THE OTTOMAN CENTURIES: THE RISE AND FALL OF THE TURKISH EMPIRE*; William Morrow; New York, 1977.

A Brief and Idiosyncratic Bibliography

Lewis, G. L.; *TEACH YOURSELF TURKISH*; David McKay; New York, 1953.

Lewis, Raphaela; *EVERYDAY LIFE IN OTTOMAN TURKEY*; G.P. Putnam's Sons; New York, 1971.

Mango, Andrew; *DISCOVERING TURKEY*; Hastings House Publishers; New York, 1971.

Morier, James; *THE ADVENTURES OF HAJJI BABA OF ISPAHAN*; reprint of the 1824 edition; Random House, Inc.; New York, 1937.

Redhouse Press; *CONTEMPORARY TURKISH-ENGLISH DICTIONARY*; Istanbul, 1983.

— *NEW REDHOUSE TURKISH-ENGLISH DICTIONARY*; Istanbul, 1968.

Stark, Freya; *ALEXANDER'S PATH*; John Murray; London, 1958.

— *RIDING TO THE TIGRIS*; Harcourt Brace and Co.; New York, 1959.

Sumner-Boyd, Hilary & Freely, John; *STROLLING THROUGH ISTANBUL*; Redhouse Press; Istanbul, 1974 (see *Blue Guide ISTANBUL* by Freely, above)

(various authors); *Guide Bleu TURQUIE*; Hachette; Paris, 1986

About the Author

Holly Chase writes and lectures on the arts, cultures, and cuisines of the Middle East and the Mediterranean. Her work has appeared in THE CHRISTIAN SCIENCE MONITOR, ANTIQUES, and GOURMET as well as in various scholarly publications.

Born and raised in Connecticut, she first went to Turkey in 1971 and lived there during the mid-1970's. As an Oriental rug dealer, tour guide, ethnographer, and culinary researcher, she continues to travel throughout Turkey: from its Balkan borders to Mesopotamia and beyond. She unpacks her bags at home in Connecticut.